Understanding Political Science Statistics Using SPSS

This manual walks students through the procedures for analysis in SPSS and provides exercises that go hand-in-hand with online data sets. The manual complements the textbook *Understanding Political Science Statistics: Observations and Expectations in Political Analysis*, by Peter Galderisi, making it easy to use alongside the book in a course or as a stand-alone guide to using SPSS. Galderisi demonstrates how to use both syntax and GUI driven formats and shows sample results of the analyses. Filled with annotated screenshots from SPSS version 22 (but compatible with all versions, including the student version), the students will be guided through standard processes replete with examples and exercises to ready them for future work in political science research.

The diverse group of data sets provided include subsamples of both the 2008 and 2012 American National Election Studies, a Eurobarometer survey, single year and longitudinal congressional district files, the 2012 Comparative Congressional Election Study data set, and a comparative, crossnational country file. Versions with reduced case numbers and variables are also included that are compatible with the student version.

This manual (and a parallel Stata manual) are available as stand-alone products or packaged with the textbook *Understanding Political Science Statistics*, and data sets are available at **www.routledge.com/cw/galderisi**.

Peter Galderisi has taught political science methods and statistics for more than three decades, and is currently a lecturer and local internship director in the Political Science Department at the University of California, San Diego. Previously, Galderisi was a Professor or Visiting Professor at Utah State, UCLA, UC Santa Cruz, and Cal State Fullerton. He specializes in U.S. political parties, campaigns and elections, American political development, interest groups, and election law.

Understanding Political Science Statistics Using SPSS

A Manual with Exercises

Peter Galderisi

Routledge
Taylor & Francis Group

NEW YORK AND LONDON

First published 2015
by Routledge
711 Third Avenue, New York, NY 10017

and by Routledge
2 Park Square, Milton Park, Abingdon, Oxon, OX14 4RN

Routledge is an imprint of the Taylor & Francis Group, an informa business

Library of Congress Cataloging-in-Publication Data
Galderisi, Peter.
  Understanding political science statistics : observations and expectations in political analysis / Peter Galderisi.
    pages cm
  1. Political statistics.   2. Political science—Statistical methods.   3. Political science—Methodology.   I. Galderisi, Peter F.   II. Title.
  JA71.7.G35 2015
  320.01'5195—dc23
  2014030207

ISBN: 978-1-138-85067-5 (pbk)

Typeset in Adobe Garamond Pro
by Apex CoVantage, LLC

Contents

Acknowledgments

SPSS software is developed and owned by the IBM Corporation: http://www.spss.com/software/statistics/

The 2008 and 2012 National Election data were made available through the American National Election Studies Organization.

> The American National Election Studies (AANES; http://www.electionstudies.org). The ANES 2008 Time Series Study [dataset]. Stanford University and the University of Michigan [producers].
>
> These materials are based on work supported by the National Science Foundation under grants SES-0535334, SES-0720428, SES-0840550, and SES-0651271, Stanford University, and the University of Michigan.
>
> The American National Election Studies (AANES; http://www.electionstudies.org). The ANES 2012 Time Series Study [dataset]. Stanford University and the University of Michigan [producers].
>
> These materials are based on work supported by the National Science Foundation under grants SES-0937727 and SES-0937715, Stanford University, and the University of Michigan.
>
> Any opinions, findings, and conclusions or recommendations expressed in these materials are those of the author(s) and do not necessarily reflect the views of the funding organizations.

The 2008 and 2008–2012 congressional district files contain information made available from the following:

> *The Daily Kos* (originally found in The Swing State Project) for results for pre and post redistricted estimates of presidential votes within each

district (http://www.dailykos.com/story/2012/11/19/1163009/-Daily-Kos-Elections-presidential-results-by-congressional-district-for-the-2012–2008-elections).

The Federal Election Commission (http://www.fec.gov) for information on voting and campaign finances.

Keith Poole (University of Georgia) for party unity and DW-Nominate scores.

George C. Edwards III (Texas A&M) for Presidential Support scores.

The American Conservative Union (ACU; http://www.conservative.org) for ideology scores and seniority data.

The U.S. Census Bureau for 2007, 2010, and 2012 estimates of demographic factors. These data were compiled using their FactFinder program with the American Community Survey 3-Year Estimates (http://www.census.gov/acs/www).

The Cook Political Report and POLIDATA for The Cook PVI scores.

The Clerk of the U.S. House (http://clerk.house.gov/member_info/electionInfo/) for verification of voting data.

Lindsay Nielson, David Todd, Jordan Hsu, and Soren Nelson (UC San Diego) for assistance with updating these data.

Eurobarometer 69:2 National and European Identity, European Elections, European Values, and Climate Change, March–May 2008:

Permission provided by the Office for Official Publications of the European Communities. Eurostat, http://ec.europa.eu/public_opinion/archives/eb/eb69/eb69_annexes.pdf, ©European Communities, 2008.

CCES2012: 2012 Cooperative Congressional Election Survey

Permission provided by the Principal Investigators of the CCES study Ansolabehere, Stephen, 2012, "CCES Common Content, 2012," http://hdl.handle.net/1902.1/21447 CCES [Distributor] V2 [Version]

CROSSNAT

Data and permissions provided by the following:

The International Institute for Democracy and Electoral Assistance, http://www.idea.int/uid/

The World Bank-Data, http://data.worldbank.org/data-catalog/world-development-indicators/wdi-2012

Terry Miller, Anthony B. Kim, and Kim R. Holmes, 2014 Index of Economic Freedom (Washington, D.C.: The Heritage Foundation and Dow Jones & Company, Inc., 2014), http://www.heritage.org/index

Freedom House, "Freedom in the World: Aggregate ans Subcategory Scores," http://www.freedomhouse.org/report/freedom-world-aggregate-and-subcategory-scores#.U-fj035EPwY

"Freedom of the Press," http://freedomhouse.org/report-types/freedom-press#.U-flIH5EPwY

General Overview
Introduction to Using SPSS for Data Analysis

SPSS is a general data manipulation and analytics program that allows people with limited or non-existent programming skills to produce some fairly sophisticated output from computer-based data sources. The following will serve as a brief primer and guide to the use of **SPSS** (the examples use version 22).

There are several ways to use the **SPSS** statistical package. They are ordered in reverse price order.

1. Purchase a full license for **SPSS 22**—over $1,000 (thought not).
2. Purchase an almost full **'GRAD PACK'** at your campus store (usually around $99 for a one-year license). This is only recommended for those individuals who will wish to continue using **SPSS** after your class is finished, e.g., for a senior thesis.
3. Purchase and download a six-month license (choose PC or Mac) for the **BASE GradPack** for about $40 from an **SPSS** educational reseller (check the Web).
4. Use **SPSS** for free in the computer lab at your campus.
5. Another option is to use the **SPSS** "Student edition" packaged with many other workbooks. This edition has many limitations. It can't utilize large data files (50 variables, 1,500 cases limit). More importantly, it neither allows syntax entry (see below) nor does it produce the syntax equivalent as part of your output if you use the graphic menu-driven interface (the **GRAD PACK** and lab versions do). This makes it difficult for your instructor to see where you might have made a mistake.

1.1 SPSS FILE TYPES

First, let's introduce the three different types of SPSS files with which you'll be working. Each type of file carries with it a certain default suffix (three letter code after the period) unless you choose to change that (I recommend against it). Each of these files will open with, but only with, the SPSS program.

*.sav This denotes a saved **SPSS** system file. This contains the data (spreadsheet), labels, and missing value parameters that are set up. In the following examples, the files that you will predominantly use are **ANES2008A.SAV** and **CONGRESS2008.SAV**.

*.sps This denotes a syntax file; i.e., a file that contains instructions for a particular analysis. This will include recodes, crosstabs, and all of the introductory information needed to access your system file. I recommend that before you exit the **SPSS** program, you save and label each syntax file that you create using a name (before the period) that reflects the analysis you are conducting, adding a number to the end indicating which run or attempt it was. For example, "age-vote1" could denote the first set of instructions that I used. **SPSS** will automatically add the .sps suffix (**age-vote1.sps**). You can then save this for future use on your drive. The computer doesn't care what name you use, but I find it easier to follow my work if I choose names that coincide with my analyses.

*.spv This denotes an output file. Although they can be read only by the **SPSS** program, parts can be directly copied and pasted into a Word document (or other word processor). They (as well as the syntax files) can also be exported in part or in their entirety into a Word, Excel, PDF, PowerPoint, or other document type using the **EXPORT** feature of the **File** command.

In the following pages, I will show how to write syntax and produce outputs using the **SPSS** statistical package. The **SPSS** Graphics User Interface (**GUI**) will also be demonstrated.

Examples will mainly be derived from the **ANES2008A.SAV** and **CONGRESS2008.SAV** data files. This will allow your instructor to use the other files for class exercises. Several suggested exercises appear at the end of each section or chapter. One set of exercises will carry through a common, progressive theme for **ANES2012A**.

Note: I believe that programs like **SPSS** are only useful if they help us to answer logically derived and developed questions. Consequently, certain exercises will be cumulative. The coding and procedures in a later section will often rely on results obtained in a previous section. I recommend keeping your work from each of these sections as you proceed through your course. For faculty wishing to have exercises that use just one of the data sets, the exercises here will be reformatted and placed on the book's website by data set.

If using **SPSS** (home or campus) you will have two options.

1. Create your instructions via a syntax window. This is much like opening up and typing within a Word document.

PROS:

> You can easily visualize the logical progression of your analysis from file retrieval, to data manipulation (operationalization), to analysis.
>
> For some procedures, especially manipulating data, it is more time efficient than using the pull-down menus.
>
> You can save the syntax in **SPSS** and open it later to redo or lightly alter your analysis.

CONS:

> Many students prefer graphic interfaces (**GUIs**) so that they may use pull-down menus rather than writing code.

2. Use the pull down menus (**GUIs**).

PROS:

> Many students prefer graphic interfaces (**GUIs**) so that they may use pull-down menus rather than writing code. For many analysis procedures, the selection of options may seem easier.
>
> You won't have to worry about making simple syntax errors (e.g., leaving a period off at the end of a procedure).

CONS:

> For some procedures, especially manipulating data, it is actually more complicated than writing syntax.
>
> It is harder to keep track of what you have been doing (although the non-student versions will print out the full syntax that corresponds to your menu-driving for your instructor to review).

The choice is yours. The following pages will demonstrate how to use the syntax-driven format, show the results of analyses, and then present a sample of the use of the **SPSS GUI** menus. All examples will use screenshots taken from analyses run on a Windows 8.1 platform—**SPSS** full version 22 (any major differences from earlier versions will be listed). A few appended notes will show differences when using a Mac.

1.2 FIRST STEPS

Downloading Data Files

All data sets will be available on the Routledge Press website. A password will be provided for each student who purchases a version of the manual. I suggest, particularly for Mac users, to download these directly to your desktop or a USB thumb drive.

Protecting Data Files

Students often make a simple mistake when transforming data, and then save the original data file with the errors included. The best way to avoid this problem is to (using old-fashioned terminology) "write protect" or set your original data files to "read only." Alternatively, one can save your altered file under a slightly different name (say **ANES2008A2.SAV** rather than **ANES2008A.SAV**) so as to differentiate the altered from the original version.

Windows (All Examples Use Windows 8.1, 64-bit)

Locate the file, and right-click on it (in this example I am working with the **ANES2008A.SAV** file located on my desktop). On the bottom of the listed menu, (1) left-click or right-click on "Properties."

A new window will open. In the "General" tab, go down to the section on "Attributes" and check off by left-clicking (2) "Read-only." Left-click (3) OK. From this point on, even if you try to change the original data file, you will be prevented from doing so.

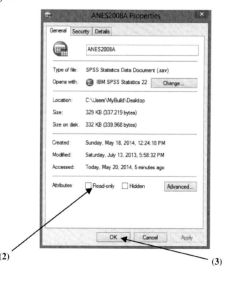

(1) (2) (3)

Mac (All Examples Use Snow Leopard OS)

Mac OS uses a slightly different method for accessing and changing file attributes. Locate the file and right-click it. A menu will appear. Click on "Get Info."

A new menu will appear. On the bottom of that menu you will find a section called "Sharing and Permissions." Open (left-click) that and, if not set already, set (left-click) each permission to "Read only." You can always create an altered file under a different name, but your original file should stay protected.

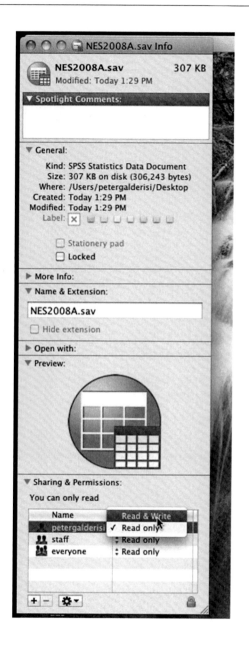

Opening a Syntax Window (All Examples Use the Full Version of SPSS 22)

Within **SPSS** (non-student version) you can type all of your instructions (syntax) as you would type up a Word document. To do so, you will need to first open a new syntax window to provide you with a blank page upon which to type.

After opening the program for the first time, you will see a blank, Excel-like spreadsheet. In Windows, (1) left-click on the "**File**" tab, (2) move the cursor to "**New**," and then move the cursor and (3) left-click "**Syntax**."

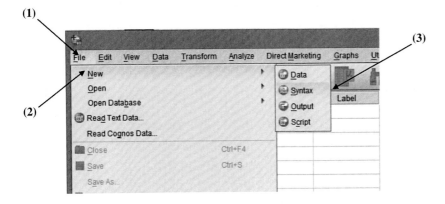

A new window will appear in which you can type your syntax instructions:

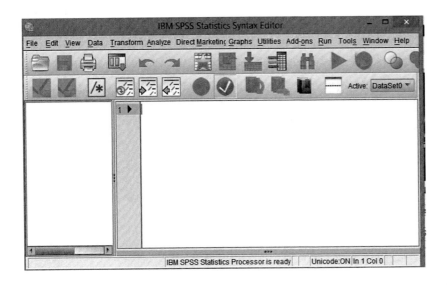

The instructions are similar for MAC OS, but the graphics will appear somewhat different (Macs have their tool bar on the top of the screen, not the top of the program page):

Instructions on syntax commands and **GUI** menus follow. At the end, you will be shown how to execute ("**Run**") your set of instructions and save them. Once you create and save your first set of syntax commands, you can then retrieve it by either left-clicking "**File**," "**Open**" (not "**New**"), syntax, or, in some setups, a list of previously used files will automatically appear when you open **SPSS**.

General Rules for Using SPSS in Syntax Mode

a. All **SPSS** commands follow the following convention. Code names that refer to the titles of the procedures you wish to use should begin in column 1 of each line (this is not a requirement, but it makes it easier for you to locate any error). The instructions that tell the program how to carry out any procedure MUST follow those procedure codes with at least one space between them. If the instructions are too lengthy to fit on one line of input (assume 80 character lines for decent viewing), they can be continued on the very next line (I recommend indenting at least two spaces). It is also easier to follow your procedures if you place each subcommand on a different line (see examples throughout the manual). Procedures with their attendant instructions MUST end with a period (otherwise the next procedure and instructions will be considered a continuation of the first).

b. To access several *variables* at once, separate each variable name by a comma or a space.

Contiguous variables can be accessed by connecting the first and last variable names with the word **TO**. As an example, turn to the example from the **ANES2008A** file codebook. If you wanted to analyze each of the thermometer items from **V15 to V19** with a similar procedure, you could either list each variable name, separated by a space and/or comma (I recommend a comma). . . .

V15, V16, V17, V18, V19

. . . or list the string of variables as:

V15 TO V19

The latter choice is preferable since you are less likely to make a typographical mistake when you have less to type. The same could be accomplished with the pull-down menu by highlighting the entire list of feeling thermometer items. Make sure, however, that you want to use all of those variables in your analysis. Also note—the **SPSS** variable item names (**V15**) are not the same as the original codebook entries (**B1a. Feeling Thermometer: President**) found in the full version of the **ANES** data file. The coding has been simplified for you.

Note: Some common errors when using syntax (**ANES2008A** file as an example):

No comma, no space
Example: **V15V16 V17 V18 V19**
Result: **SPSS** will not be able to execute the procedure because it won't be able to find a variable named *V15V16*

Comma where it doesn't belong
Example: **V15, TO, V19**
Result: **SPSS** will not be able to execute the procedure because it won't be able to find a variable named *TO*

Note: **SPSS** isn't case specific. *V15* and *TO* or *v15* and *to* are interchangeable.

c. The rules for dealing with *values* or categories within variables are similar. Discrete values can be listed separated by commas or spaces. Contiguous values can be listed by connecting the first and last relevant value with the word **THRU** or a simple dash (-). The lowest value can be referred to as **LO**, the highest as **HI**. For example, refer to **V4** (age) in your **ANES2008A** codebook. If you wished to combine (e.g., by way of a **RECODE**) all those individuals under 30 years of age, you could either list the entries separately. . . .

18,19,20,21,22,23,24,25,26,27,28,29

. . . or contiguously:

18 THRU 29

or

18–29

Note: The same error applies to adding a comma to the second choice.

18,THRU,29

SPSS will return an error message stating that numeric and string (**THRU**) values cannot be combined.

On the other hand, if you leave out a comma or space in the value listing (**1819, 20**) **SPSS** will just ignore the **1819** and work with the other values. The values **18** and **19** will still be treated separately.

d. Within any procedure, unrelated sets of instructions can be added by separating the entries with a */*. Alternately, one can respecify the procedure name in column 1 with the related instruction separated by at least one space (see the section on **RECODES** for an example). Sometimes, as in the example I will show, typographical inefficiency may help us to keep our analysis in logical order. Use whichever is best for you.

General Rules for Using SPSS in GUI (MENU) Mode

Setting up your data analysis in SPSS follows many of the same rules as you would use in other computer programs. The following names will be used consistently throughout this volume:

Left-click: to open a data set, choose a procedure, or choose an option.

Select variable: each operationalization, selection, or analysis procedure will have a blank box in which you will place your variable(s). The variable list will be presented on the left of the procedures dialogue box.

To move a specific variable into the appropriate blank box, any of the following techniques can be used:

1. Move your cursor down to the appropriate variable from the list, left-click on that variable, and, using your mouse, slide it over into the appropriate box. To remove that variable from the selection box, left-click on it and slide it back into the variable list.
2. Move your cursor down to the appropriate variable from the list, left-click on that variable, and then left-click on the arrow button:

To remove that variable from the selection box, left-click on it and left-click on the reverse arrow button:

3. Limited option: Move your cursor down to the appropriate variable from the list and double left-click it. This method is only applicable to procedures where only one blank variable box exists. It cannot be used for any procedure where different boxes exist for independent and dependent variables, analysis variables, and selection criteria based upon categories of a second variable, etc.

CONTENTS

Setting Up the SPSS Data File for Analysis

Three paths exist to open any data file. One can double left-click on that file and, if the **SPSS** program is on the computer, the file will automatically open (much like clicking on a Word document will automatically open it in Word).

A second method is to open up the **SPSS** program, left-click on "**File**," then slide the cursor to "**Open**," then "**Data**" (the same menu as you used for your syntax) and left-click it.

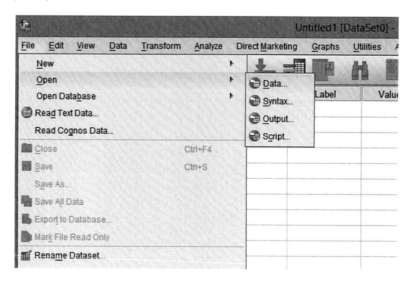

A new window will pop up, allowing you to locate your data set. Again, in this example, the data set is on my desktop.

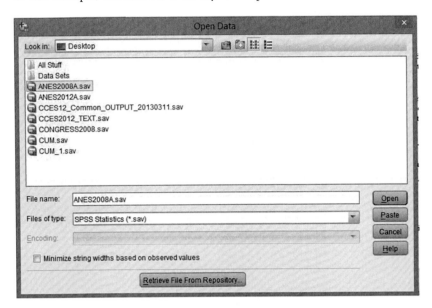

Move the cursor to the data set you wish to use and left-click "**Open**." The empty spreadsheet should be populated with the data for this file.

2.1 GET FILE

Another method is to retrieve the file through a syntax procedure **GET FILE**. On my computer, the full **ANES2008A SPSS** file (**ANES2008A.sav**) is on my desktop. My procedure would be:

GET FILE='C:\Users\MyBuild\Desktop\ANES2008A.sav'.

File names must be enclosed between apostrophes. End the **GET** procedure with a period *after* the closing apostrophe. If you are using a CD or USB thumb drive, and you haven't placed your file in a subdirectory, your **GET** procedure will be much easier to type out.

For example, if the USB drive on the computer you are using (as an example) is the "G" drive, then your procedure should be:

GET FILE='G:\ANES2008A.sav'.

Warning: If you make a copy of the data set (**ANES2008A.SAV**) or any other, make sure to lock or write protect (read only) the file (see pp. 4–5).

2.2 WEIGHT

Some data sets try to but don't achieve a true random sample. Additionally, some groups might be purposely oversampled in order to have a large enough size for each group to analyze. For example, in the semiannual Eurobarometer surveys, approximately 1,000 individuals are sampled in each country in order to guarantee a large enough sample for each. But if you want to analyze Europe as a whole, you wouldn't want the sample of citizens from the small country of Luxembourg to count as much as the citizens from France. Before doing any further analysis, one needs to readjust the subsample sizes to better approximate what they would look like if the sample were purely random, or equiprobable. This readjustment is done using the **WEIGHT** command. Just follow the command with one of the weight variables listed in your codebook. Weights are discussed further in the text, Chapter 4, the section "A Summary Example with Aggregated Data," Chapter 6, the section "Considerations in Sampling," and elsewhere in the end of chapter exercises.

For example, to use the standard **ANES2008A** supplied weight (**PW**), the procedure is as follows:

Weight by PW.

This weight adjusts for the unintentional oversampling of wealthy and highly educated individuals. In 2008, an adjustment was also made to compensate for the intentional oversampling of Blacks and Hispanics (a large enough subsample was viewed as important). Both adjustments are made by placing each group in line with their proportions in the full U.S. Census.

Some analysts have been concerned with the unintentional, but consistent throughout the years, oversampling of women. I've made an adjustment (again, using Census estimates) for the real proportion of men and women 18 years and older. If you prefer to include that adjustment together with the others then just use the following, as I have done with the examples in this manual.

Weight by PW2.

Note that this adjustment is included in the single weight variable for the 2012 **ANES** data file (**PW2012**).

The **GUI** procedure for incorporating a weight is as follows. As with most procedures, a list of variables from the opened data file will be presented for selection.

Step 1: From either the output viewer page (you've already opened the data set), or the data editor page (spreadsheet), left-click on the **Data** tab.

Step 2: Move down the drop down list and left-click on "**Weight cases**."

Step 3: You should see the following:

Choose (left-click) the "**Weight cases by**" option.

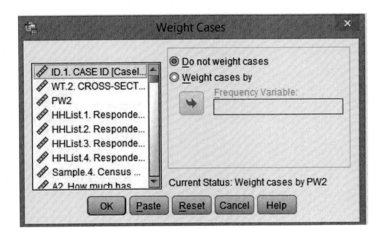

Step 4: Left-click on the variable you wish to use to weight your cases (in our example, **PW2**). Either drag (hold down the left-clicker while doing so) to the "**Frequency Variable**" window, double-click on the variable, or left-click on the arrow to the left of that window. Click the "**OK**" tab.

If, for any reason, you are not sure if you assigned a weight, repeat Steps 1 and 2. You will be able to tell whether or not a weight is applied. Note that for true random samples (if possible) and complete population data sets (for example, a file of congressional data for one year), no weight needs to be applied and won't appear in your codebook.

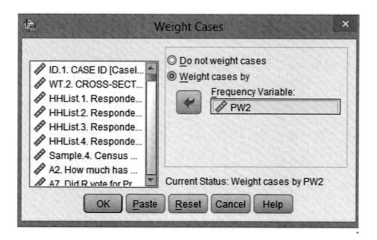

We are now ready to begin some data manipulation and analysis.

Commonly Used SPSS Commands— Operationalization

The term *operationalization* has to do with going from a concept (say, distrust of a certain group, how one voted, etc.) to a measurement. The first stage in operationalizing a concept is to choose the variable or variables that one might use. Sometimes that is sufficient. Often, however, we either need to manipulate categories (to make certain types of analyses easier and to increase categorical sample sizes), or combine variables to match our idea of our original concept. If we are using variables as single operationalizations, then a **RECODE** procedure is the most useful.

Even though you run one of the following "manipulation" or operationalization commands, no output (other than a generated listing of the syntax equivalent) will be shown until you run an analysis procedure (Chapter 4). For that reason, you would want to read the section on **FREQUENCIES** (Chapter 4.1) so that you can see the results of your operationalizations.

For demonstration purposes, each of these operationalizations was followed by the following. The **FREQUENCIES** procedure will be further discussed in Chapter 4.1:

FREQUENCIES VARIABLES = variable or variable list.

3.1 RECODE

Function: reclassifies the values (categories) of a variable in order to reduce the number of categories or better approximate your conceptualization.

For more on this topic, see Chapter 2, "Measuring Properties and the Importance of Categorization," and Exercise 9, in *Understanding Political Science Statistics: Observations and Expectations in Political Analysis.*

RECODE variable(s) (value or value list=new value)
(value or value list=new value)(repeat as necessary).

Example 3.1—For all data files, a generic missing value code of **SYSMIS**. If, for example, using the **CONGRESS2008** data set, you wish to eliminate from your analysis those districts where an incumbent was not running (open seat), you would need only to recode the unwanted response to a **SYSMIS**.

RECODE INC08 (3, 4=SYSMIS).

Before **RECODE**

FREQUENCIES VARIABLES=INC08.

Inc08

		Frequency	Percent	Valid Percent	Cumulative Percent
Valid	1	229	52.6	52.6	52.6
	2	170	39.1	39.1	91.7
	3	7	1.6	1.6	93.3
	4	29	6.7	6.7	100.0
	Total	435	100.0	100.0	

RECODE Inc08 (3, 4=SYSMIS).
FREQUENCIES VARIABLES=INC08.

Note that **SPSS** is not case sensitive. **Inc08** is the same as **INC08**

After **RECODE**

Inc08

		Frequency	Percent	Valid Percent	Cumulative Percent
Valid	1	229	52.6	57.4	57.4
	2	170	39.1	42.6	100.0
	Total	399	91.7	100.0	
Missing	System	36	8.3		
Total		435	100.0		

Notice that the 36 non-incumbents (categories 3 and 4) are now listed as missing and would not be included in any analysis where **Inc08** was used.

Example 3.2—What if you wanted a simple two-category analysis where you want to separate those districts in which Obama exceeded his national vote (52.9%) from those where he did not?

RECODE OBAMA (lo thru 52.9 = 1)(53 thru hi = 2).

As **OBAMA** has been rounded to a whole percentage, 101 categories are possible before recoding (0–100). In actuality, the percentages range from 22 to 95. After recoding, you would only have two categories:

RECODE OBAMA (lo thru 52.9 = 1)(53 thru hi = 2).
FREQUENCIES VARIABLES=OBAMA.

After **RECODE**

Obama

		Frequency	Percent	Valid Percent	Cumulative Percent
Valid	1	225	51.7	51.7	51.7
	2	210	48.3	48.3	100.0
	Total	435	100.0	100.0	

Caution:

If your file contains a negative value coded as a missing value (no appropriate answer), don't use **lo** but rather the actual lowest value. For example, if a –9 (rather than **SYSMIS**) was assigned to those who wouldn't specify their income, then starting a **RECODE** field with **lo** would include those non-responders in the low-income category. None of the data sets in this manual have negative numbers, but you may create a variable that does.

Example 3.3—Return to the **ANES2008A** file. Maybe you are not concerned about "how Democratic" or "Republican" one is—just whether they are on one side or the other.

RECODE V36 (0 1 2 =1)(3 = 2)(4 5 6 = 3).

Categories can be separated by commas or spaces. Also note that, in this recode, only "pure independents" (value = 3) are treated as independents. If you believe that "independent leaners" should also be treated as "independents," the recode becomes:

RECODE V36 (0 1 =1)(2 3 4= 2)(5 6 = 3).

If you wished to specify only the intensity of one's partisan preference without regard to partisan *direction* (e.g., to address the hypothesis "the more partisan one is, the more likely one is to vote"), then recode as follows (3 would be the most partisan here).

RECODE V36 (2 3 4 = 1)(1 5 = 2)(0 6 = 3).

Before **RECODE**

FREQUENCIES VARIABLES=V36.

V36 Party ID Summary

		Frequency	Percent	Valid Percent	Cumulative Percent
Valid	0	386	18.4	18.6	18.6
	1	316	15.0	15.2	33.9
	2	342	16.3	16.5	50.4
	3	238	11.3	11.5	61.9
	4	247	11.7	11.9	73.8
	5	273	13.0	13.2	87.0
	6	270	12.9	13.0	100.0
	Total	2072	98.6	100.0	
Missing	System	30	1.4		
Total		2102	100.0		

After **RECODE**

RECODE V36 (0 1 2 =1)(3 = 2)(4 5 6 = 3).
FREQUENCIES VARIABLES=V36.

V36 Party ID Summary

		Frequency	Percent	Valid Percent	Cumulative Percent
Valid	1	1044	49.7	50.4	50.4
	2	238	11.3	11.5	61.9
	3	790	37.6	38.1	100.0
	Total	2072	98.6	100.0	
Missing	System	30	1.4		
Total		2102	100.0		

RECODE V36 (0 1 =1)(2 3 4= 2)(5 6 = 3).
FREQUENCIES VARIABLES=V36.

V36 Party ID Summary

		Frequency	Percent	Valid Percent	Cumulative Percent
Valid	1	702	33.4	33.9	33.9
	2	827	39.4	39.9	73.8
	3	543	25.9	26.2	100.0
	Total	2072	98.6	100.0	
Missing	System	30	1.4		
Total		2102	100.0		

RECODE V36 (2 3 4 = 1)(1 5 = 2)(0 6 = 3).
FREQUENCIES VARIABLES=V36.

V36 Party ID Summary

		Frequency	Percent	Valid Percent	Cumulative Percent
Valid	1	827	39.4	39.9	39.9
	2	589	28.0	28.4	68.3
	3	656	31.2	31.7	100.0
	Total	2072	98.6	100.0	
Missing	System	30	1.4		
Total		2102	100.0		

Caution:

Without recoding into a new variable, or specifying **TEMPORARY** before each of the previous three recodes, running all three **V36 RECODES** within one analysis will lead to erroneous results. The first **RECODE** leaves us with 3 categories of **Party ID**. Following with the second will leave us with only 2 (categories 5 and 6 no longer exist and thus no category 3 is possible). The new category 2 will be comprised of the old categories 2 and 3. This is probably the most common type of mistake that students make.

Example 3.4—The previous example demonstrates that the **RECODE** command not only simplifies some analysis but also allows us to use the same variable (**V36**) to measure two different concepts (partisan *direction* and partisan *intensity*). If you are doing both in the same run, I recommend adding the following to the **RECODE** command.

INTO new variable.

The following two lines would create a separate variable (**V36P, V36S**) for "direction of partisanship" and "strength of partisanship" separate from the original variable, **V36** (which would maintain its original coding):

RECODE V36 (0 1 2 =1)(3 = 2)(4 5 6 = 3) INTO V36P.
RECODE V36 (2 3 4 = 1)(1 5 = 2)(0 6 = 3) INTO V36S.

As an alternative, you can precede each recode with the **TEMPORARY** command. After executing a procedure (like **FREQUENCIES**), the variable will revert to its original full categorization, ready to be recoded again.

TEMPORARY.
RECODE V36 (0 1 2 =1)(3 = 2)(4 5 6 = 3).
FREQUENCIES VARIABLES=V36.
TEMPORARY.
RECODE V36 (2 3 4 = 1)(1 5 = 2)(0 6 = 3).
FREQUENCIES VARIABLES=V36.

Example 3.5—The **RECODE** command can also be used to create an *entirely new* variable not related to what already exists in the file. For example, what if we wanted to attach to each respondent's listing the type of electoral system under which they are governed (see the **EURO69** codebook). The International Institute for Democracy and Electoral Assistance (**IDEA**) classifies countries into three general election rule types: (1) Single Member District, (2) Mixed, and (3) Proportional (additional variations are listed for each—see codebook). One could then create a new variable (e.g., **ETYPE**) from the existing variable (**COUNTRY**) by recoding each set of countries into their respective election system.

RECODE COUNTRY (8, 9, 16, 17, 24 = 1)
(3, 4, 21, 23 = 2)(ELSE=3) into ETYPE.

Caution:

I generally don't suggest using the **ELSE** specification because depending on which version of SPSS you are using, it might include missing values. For this survey, however, there are no missing values for **COUNTRY**.

Before the recode, 29 country codes would be presented. After the recode, these three (**data WEIGHT=W27**) would appear:

RECODE COUNTRY (8, 9, 16, 17, 24 = 1)
(3, 4, 21, 23 = 2)(ELSE=3) into ETYPE.
FREQUENCIES VARIABLES=COUNTRY.

		Frequency	Percent	Valid Percent	Cumulative Percent
Valid	1.00	6596	24.8	24.8	24.8
	2.00	4480	16.8	16.8	41.6
	3.00	15563	58.4	58.4	100.0
	Total	26640	100.0	100.0	

You will be shown how to add category names (**SMD, MIXED, PR**) to the table in Chapter 5.

Example 3.6—When deciding how to reclassify or recode information, two common methods are used. The first is preferable, the second might be necessary. This will be discussed more in your course. Conceptually, and based upon sound theoretical judgment, how would you like to reclassify categories? Return to the **ANES2008A** file. Conceptually, you may wish to collapse the categories of those variables indicating approval or disapproval of former President Bush's handling of the economy into three possibilities (Approve/Neutral/Disapprove).

RECODE V11 (1 2=1)(3=2)(4 5=3).

But you might find that you will have few individuals in the recoded "Approve" category (1). Sometimes, in order to have enough cases in any grouping, we must fall back onto an alternate reclassification. Here are the original percentages (weighted by **PW2**):

1. Approve strongly   7.6%
2. Approve not strongly   10.6%
3. Neither/DK   3.3%
4. Disapprove not strongly 16.9%
5. Disapprove strongly   61.5%

Given how few survey respondents approved of the president's handling of the economy, you might decide to split individuals into two groups, "Disapprove strongly" or "Not." The recode would then be as follows:

RECODE V11 (1 2 3 4=1)(5=2).

Note:
Characters like . . .

,   /   =   (   )

. . . are considered delimiters. Delimiters set off whatever is around them and can be surrounded by a space or spaces or no spaces at all.

Also:

Recoding a value into itself (0 1 2 = 1), as was demonstrated in Example 3.3, isn't really necessary, but listing it would cause no harm, and it might help you to guarantee that all of your categories have been covered. It also must be done when creating a new variable via the **INTO** convention (otherwise those non-listed categories will be eliminated). Also, when using the **GUI**, all original values must be included.

Example 3.7—Separate recodes can be performed within the same procedure command (rather than respecifying **RECODE** on another line):

RECODE INC08 (3, 4=SYSMIS)
/OBAMA (lo thru 52.9 = 1)(53 thru hi = 2).

On the other hand, with so little to type, and with computers being fast these days, you might just want to enter the separate **RECODE** commands, each followed by a ".". This will keep your operationalizations separate to coincide with your thought process. It's up to you.

However, if several variables are to be recoded the same way, there is no need to repeat the value alteration instructions. For example, to recode the entire list of feeling thermometer (**V15 to V19**) scores into just three categories—cold, neutral, warm (the following is only one type of breakdown):

RECODE V15 to V19 (0 thru 40=1)(41 thru 59=2)(60 THRU 100=3).

Question: What if, as in the "partisan intensity" example, one wanted to separate those individuals with extreme (low or high) feelings from those more neutral?

Note: As mentioned, you will not see the results of any recode or new variable in your spreadsheet or output until you run an analytic procedure (**FREQUENCIES, MEANS,** etc.). Occasionally, with older versions of **SPSS**, an execution of **SPSS** will have a glitch that requires you also to type the following command before that analytic procedure.

EXECUTE.

The **GUI** procedure for the following recode follows. Notice the number of steps required. Also note that once you **RECODE** by way of a set of pull-down menus, the recoding scheme *will remain for the next variable you wish to recode.* The instructions to reset the **RECODE** procedure appears at the end of this section.

To **RECODE** into the same variable (Example 3.3):

RECODE V36 (0 1 2 =1)(3 = 2)(4 5 6 = 3).

From any screen (output, syntax, data editor), (1) left-click on "**Transform**," then (2) move down and left-click on "**Recode into Same Variables.**" The following screen will appear:

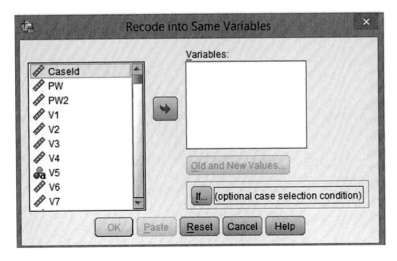

Move down and locate variable **V36** (**Party ID Summary**).

Note: If your listing has variable labels rather than names (as seen above), you can hold your cursor over each variable and the variable name will appear. Or, if you can stretch the box far enough horizontally, the variable name will be listed at the end of the label.

Alternatively, you can display the variable names by (1) left-clicking on the **"Edit"** tab and (2) moving down to and left-clicking **"Options."**

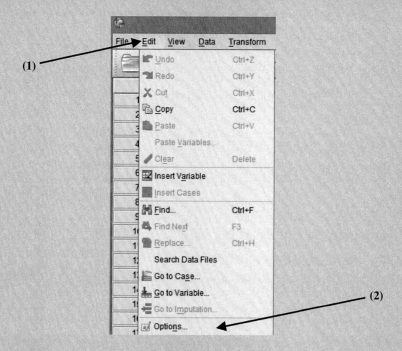

The following screen will appear. If **"Display labels"** is marked, left-click on **"Display names"** and then left-click **"OK."** If you are given a warning prompt, left-click **"OK."**

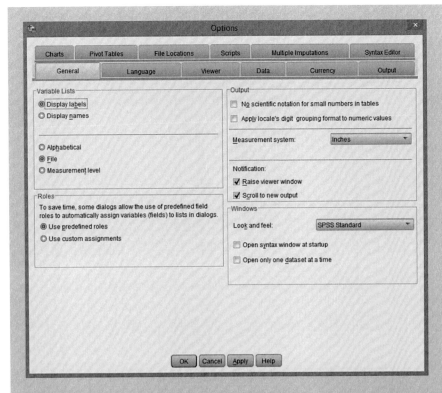

Going through the steps to pull up the **RECODE** dialog box, you will now see the following:

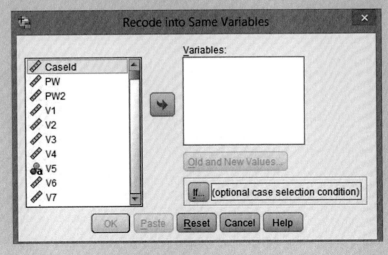

All subsequent examples will use this cleaner format.

Step 3: Left-click on the variable (**V36**) and drag it to the blank screen to the left or left-click on the arrow key. Alternatively, double click on the variable name. Once you do so, you will then be able to begin your recode process.

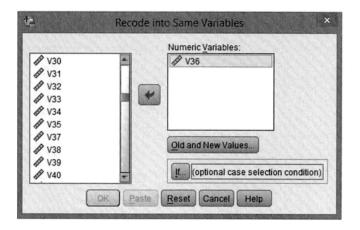

Step 4: Left-click "**OK**." The following will appear:

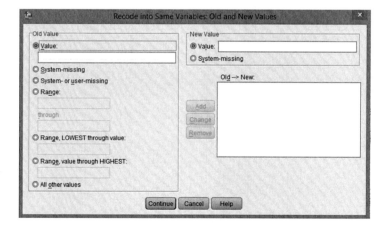

The number of subsets will depend on how you intend to recode.

You can now use any of the "**Old Value**" methods to recode **V36**. The first is rather simple as the original values to be recoded are consecutive. For this you can use the "**Range**" option.

a.   Left-click on "**Range**." Two entry boxes should turn white.
b.   Type the lowest number in your range (1) into the first box, your highest number (3) into the second.

c. Type the new value (what you want to recode the old values into) in the New Value "**value**" box (1).

d. Left-click the "**Add**" button.

You should then see the following:

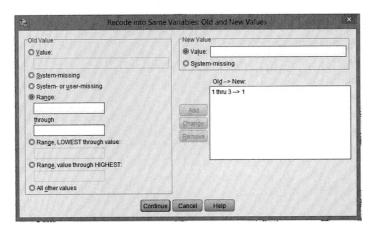

Continue with the rest of the recode ("**Old value**", "**New value**" "**Add**") until you have exhausted all possibilities. For your example, you should have two additional steps (**4→2, 3 thru 5→3**).

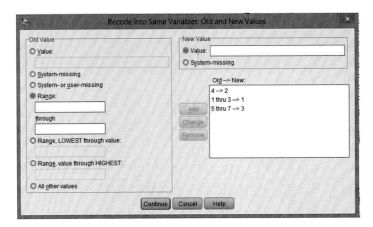

Step 5: Left-click on "**Continue.**" The original (Step 2) table should appear. Left-click on "**OK.**"

If you performed these steps properly, you will now have only three categories for **V36**.

To **RECODE** into a different variable (Example 3.3):

RECODE V36 (0 1 2 =1)(3 = 2)(4 5 6 = 3) INTO V36P.

As you did before, (1) left-click on "**Transform**" but then move down and (2) left-click on "**Recode into Different Variables**." The following screen will appear:

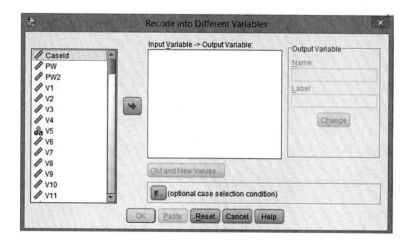

Move down the variable list and find **V36**.

Step 3: Left-click on the variable, and drag it to the blank screen to the left or left-click on the arrow key. Alternatively, double click on the variable name.

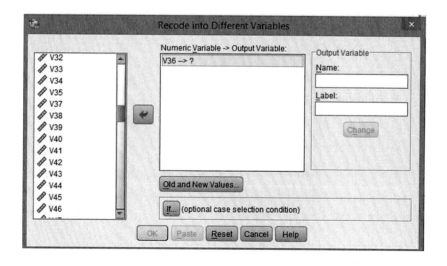

Step 3a: Type in the new variable name into the **Output Variable "Name"** field. You can also type in a label. Left-click "**Change**." Then

left-click on the "**Old and New Values**" tab. Continue with Steps 4–6 as above.

If you performed these steps properly, you will notice that a new variable and column have been added to your data spreadsheet (**V36P**).

Using the **GUI** method for recoding can be more or less arduous than what we have just demonstrated. If recoding into a new variable, just remember that you must include all the old values, *even if they are to remain the same* in the newly, recoded one. Otherwise, all unrecoded values will be assigned as "**Missing**." If you are not recoding into a new variable, however, the old values will remain as is.

To maintain the same values for both the old and new variable, left-click on "**All Other Values**" and then left-click on "**Copy Old Value(s)**." I normally warn against this method (including the use of "**ELSE**" in syntax mode), preferring that students make sure that they have recoded and can see those recodes for all values.

To eliminate certain categories (values) for your analysis, use any of the left-sided selections, then left-click "**System-missing**."

Note: Before you can recode another variable with a different recoding scheme, you will need to undo your original recode (not necessary using syntax mode). This requires removing the old variable (double left-clicking, moving, left-click, and backwards arrow), repeating Step 3, and, after opening up the **"Old and New Values"** dialog box, left clicking on *each* transformation (e.g., **1 thru 3→1**) and left-clicking the **"REMOVE"** button. This is another reason why certain transformations are easier to accomplish through the syntax method.

RECODE: Sample Exercises

Follow any **RECODE** with a simple **FREQUENCIES** procedure of the recoded variable in order to see your results:

FREQUENCIES VARIABLES=variable selected.

ANES2012A

For each exercise, weight the sample by **PW2012**.

1. Recode Age (**V4**) into four categories:

    18–30
    31–50
    51–64
    65–90

    Your first category should contain 447 or 22.4% of all valid cases.

2. Recode Marital Status (**V60**) into a new variable, **V60A**, with those who are married or widowed into a new category 1, all others listed into category 2.

    Your first category should contain 59.3% of all valid cases.

3. Recode **V13** (Approve/disapprove President's handling of health care) into three categories: those who have strong feelings of approval or disapproval (1,5), those with more moderate feelings (2,4) and those who have no opinion (3).

    Your first category should contain 72.4% of all valid cases. What does this tell you about Americans' views about health care?

CONGRESS2008–2012

No weight required as these represent entire populations.

1. Recode Incumbency Status (**INC**) for any or all (separately) of the three years to separate Incumbent (1,2) from Non-Incumbent (open=3,4) races.

    Your incumbent category should contain 399 or 91.7% of all districts in 2008.

2. Recode any Per Capita Income (**PCI**) into two categories, those under the national mean and those above. The national means are as follows (not adjusted for inflation):

    2008 $27,466
    2010 $26,952
    2012 $27,385

    Your first category should contain 68.3% of all districts in 2008.

3. Recode any Winning Percentage (**WV**) into a new variable, **SAFE**, with three categories:

    Those who won with less than 55% of the vote
    Those who won with 55.1 to 60% of the vote
    Those who won with better than 60% of the vote

    In 2008, 68.7% won by more than 60%. What does this tell you about the level of competition in congressional elections?

EURO69

For each exercise, weight the sample by **W27**. If analyzing only one country or comparing just two countries against each other, use **W1**.

1. Recode **COUNTRY** into three categories (see note 1 at end of **EURO69** codebook for electoral system type):

    Single Member District
    Mixed
    Proportional Representation

    Your first category should contain roughly one-quarter of all cases.

2. Recode **V20** (Globalization-Threat to National Culture) into a new variable, **V20A**, with three new categories: Strongly or Somewhat Agree (1), Don't Know (2), and Somewhat or Strongly Disagree (3).

    Your first category of **V20A** should contain 40.0% of all valid cases.

3. Recode **V25** (IDEOLOGICAL PLACEMENT) into two categories: all left, 1–5 (1), all right, 6–10 (2). By using **SYSMIS**, eliminate categories 11 and 12.

Your first category should contain 62.3% of all valid cases. What does this tell you about the ideological placement of Europeans in 2008?

4. Recode all three EU Proposal questions (**V16, V17, V18**), and the three Voice questions (**V11, V12, V13**) removing the **DK** category from each (**SYSMIS**).

CCES2012

For each exercise, weight the sample by **WEIGHT**.

1. Recode Education (**V2**) into three categories:

≤HS
Some or 2-year college
4-year or post grad

Your first category should contain 21,838 or 40.0% of all valid cases.

2. Recode V8 (Party ID) into three new variables:

PID1   All Democrats (1–3)
Pure Independents (4)
All Republicans (5–7)

PID2   All Democrats except non-leaners (1,2)
Leaners and Independents (3,4,5)
All Republicans except non-leaners (6,7)

PID3   All strong partisans (1,7)
Not very strong partisans (2,6)
All leaners and independents (3,4,5)

Your first category should contain 50.6%, 33.8%, and 38.6% of all valid cases, respectively.

3. Recode **V28, V29**, and **V30** each into two categories: approve, disapprove. Compare the three new breakdowns. In particular, is there a difference between one's approval of Congress as an institution and one's individual member?

CROSSNAT

No weight required as these represent entire populations.

1. Recode **IDEA_ESP** so that you separate countries that have a presidential system from those that do not. Presidential systems should exist in 101 or 51% of all valid cases.
2. Recode Percentage Turnout **VAP-President (IDEA_VAP_PR)** into two categories: those with turnout below the mean of all countries with listed data, and those above (the mean is 61.4%). You should have a slight majority with turnout above the mean.

3.2 COMPUTE

Function: creates a new variable from some combination of two or more other variables. Useful when creating multi-variable scales or difference measures that better approximate the concepts we are trying to measure.

For more on this topic, see Chapter 2, "From Nominal to Interval Data," in *Understanding Political Science Statistics: Observations and Expectations in Political Analysis*, which gives a brief discussion of creating a scale from several variables.

> **COMPUTE new variable=arithmetic expression, usually containing existing variable(s).**

Example 3.8—To create a variable (**IDEODIFF**) assessing the difference between feelings toward Liberals and Conservatives (**ANES2008A**).

> **COMPUTE IDEODIFF= V75-V76.**

IDEODIFF would range from −100 (pro-*Conservative*) to 100 (pro-*Liberal*). Note that a 0 indicates equal warmth (at any level), not necessarily chilliness toward both. Unless you are doing a means, correlation, or regression analysis, you will probably want to recode this variable into fewer categories (pro-Cons/same/pro-Lib).

Unlike most other procedures, a **COMPUTE** can only entertain one calculation. Other computations (e.g., other thermometer scale differences) would have to be defined with a second **COMPUTE** command (no commas or slashes). If, for example, you also wished to compute a difference scale for racial feelings (Whites-Blacks), then you would need two separate commands:

> **COMPUTE IDEODIFF = V75-V76.**
> **COMPUTE RACEDIFF = V80-V78.**

Example 3.9—to create a scale (e.g., **DAFFECT**) that indicates how many of the four variable items one answered for which one had a positive affect toward the Democratic Party candidate (Obama):

COMPUTE DAFFECT = V23 + V24 + V25+ V26.

This will produce a new variable (**DAFFECT**) that will range from "0" (no positive affect) to "4" (positive on all aspects). Any respondent with a missing value for any of the four original variables will be counted as missing on the new variable **DAFFECT**. Note also that, according to the codebook, categories "yes" and "no" are in different orders depending on whether they represent a positive or negative "affect."

COMPUTE DAFFECT = V23 + V24 + V25+ V26.
FREQUENCIES VARIABLES=DAFFECT.

No positive affect characteristics for Obama

DAFFECT

		Frequency	Percent	Valid Percent	Cumulative Percent
Valid	.00	238	11.3	11.6	11.6
	1.00	286	13.6	13.9	25.5
	2.00	424	20.2	20.6	46.0
	3.00	478	22.7	23.2	69.2
	4.00	634	30.2	30.8	100.0
	Total	2060	98.0	100.0	
Missing	System	42	2.0		
Total		2102	100.0		

Positive affect listed for all characteristics for Obama

Try this:
Create a scale indicating whether one was more positively inclined (affect) towards the Democratic or the Republican presidential candidate.
   Your values should range from –4 to +4
   What would a "0" mean?

Example 3.10—Using the **CONGRESS2008** file, create a variable that indicates the difference in spending between the Republican and Democratic candidates.

COMPUTE SPENDDIFF=RH$08 — DH$08.

The new variable (**SPENDIFF**) will be negative if the Democratic candidate spent more than the Republican, positive if he/she spent less, "0" if spending was equal.

Caution:

One might wish to consider creating a ratio: Democratic Spending divided by Republican Spending. The concept makes sense, but, as is often the case, if no Republican candidate ran, RH$ would equal $0, and the division cannot be calculated (any number divided by **0** = ∞).

Note: All standard arithmetic expressions can be used, including the following:

$$+ \quad - \quad / \quad x \quad \textbf{ABS (absolute value)} \quad \textbf{SQRT (square root)}$$

The **GUI** menu procedure for a **COMPUTE** is rather straightforward and allows you to use a calculator-like approach to creating your compute statement. Let's use the last example. Remember to first open the **CONGRESS2008** data set:

Step 1: From any **SPSS** window, left-click on "**Transform**," slide your cursor down to the first entry, "**Compute variable**," and left-click it. The following should appear:

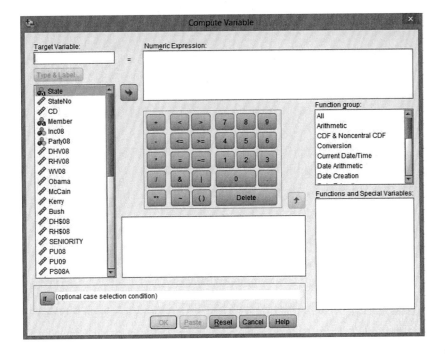

Step 2: Type in the new variable ("**Target variable**") name (**SPENDDIFF**).
Step 3: In the "**Numeric Expression**" field click/arrow, double left-click, or drag the first variable of the equation (**DH$08**). Left-click on the "–" button. Drag or double left-click **RH$08** into the end of the equation.

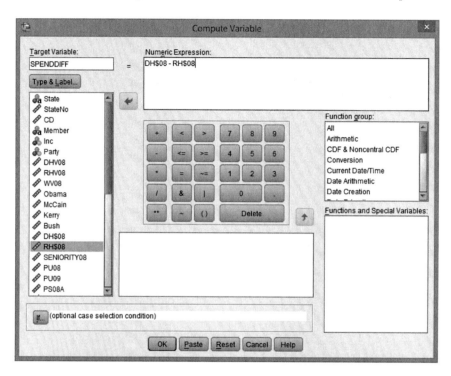

Step 4: Left-click "**OK**." Note that a new variable and data column, **SPENDDIFF**, has been added to your file.

COMPUTE: Sample Exercises

Follow any **COMPUTE** with a simple **FREQUENCIES** procedure of the computed variable in order to see your results:

FREQUENCIES VARIABLES=variable selected.

ANES2012A

For each exercise, weight the sample by **PW2012**.

1. Create a new variable, **IDEODIFF,** that measures the difference in feeling thermometer ratings of liberals and conservatives. Using the frequencies

command with tables suppressed (**FORMAT=NOTABLE**), produce the median and mean of **IDEODIFF**. What do those values tell you?

2. Create a new variable, **PRESAPPROVE**, creating a scale of presidential approval by adding the following: **V10, V11, V12, V13, V14**. Your lowest value should be 5 (approve on all counts), your highest 25 (disapprove on all counts). Produce the frequency distribution, along with the mode, median, and mean for **PRESAPPROVE**.

Congress2008–2012

1. Create a new variable, **SPENDDIFF,** that, for any year, measures the difference Democratic and Republican candidate expenditures (e.g., **DHE08-RHE08**). Using the frequencies command with tables suppressed (**FORMAT=NOTABLE**), produce the median and mean of **SPENDDIFF**. What do those values tell you?

2. Create a new variable, **WINDIFF,** that, for any year, measures the difference between the Democratic House vote and the Republican House vote (e.g., **DHV08-RHV08**). Using the frequencies command with tables suppressed (**FORMAT=NOTABLE**), produce the median and mean of **WINDIFF**. What do those values tell you? Also produce a HISTOGRAM of those values.

3. Create a new variable, **DEMDIFF,** that measures the difference between the Democratic House vote in 2010 and 2008. Using the frequencies command with tables suppressed (**FORMAT=NOTABLE**), produce the median and mean of **DEMDIFF**. What do those values tell you? Also produce a HISTOGRAM of those values.

4. Repeat #3 for 2012 versus 2008.

EURO69

For each exercise, weight the sample by **W27**. If analyzing only one country or comparing just two countries against each other, use **W1**.

1. Create a new variable, **EUPOLICY**, that creates a scale measuring support toward common EU policies. Use the three recoded variables (**V16, V17, V18**) from **RECODE** (4) above (**DK** eliminated). Your scale should range from supportive on all three counts (3) to not supportive on all three (6), with numbers in between corresponding to categories of support for at least one policy but not all.

2. Create a new variable, **EUVOICE** that creates a scale measuring political efficacy when assessing the **EU**. Use the recoded variables (**V11, V13**) from **RECODE** (4) above. Your scale should range from fully efficacious (2) to fully non-efficacious (4) with a 3 implying efficacy only for oneself or one's country, but not both. Produce the frequency distribution, along with the mode.

CCES2012

For each exercise, weight the sample by **WEIGHT**.

1. Create a new variable, **ODIFF,** that measures the absolute value of the difference between a respondent's self-placement (**V48**) and his/her placement of President Obama (**V49**) ideologically. Create a similar variable, **RDIFF**, that measures the absolute value of the difference between self-placement and placement of Governor Romney.
2. Create a new variable, **PROXIMITY**, that measures the difference between your two new variables (**ODIFF-RDIFF**). What does a negative number mean? 0? A positive number?

CROSSNAT

1. Compute the difference between the infant mortality rates of males (**WDI_IMM**) and females (**WDI_IMF**). Create a new variable **IMDIFF**. Suppressing the frequency distribution (**FORMAT=NOTABLE**), compute the median and mean. What do those values tell you? Notably, in only one country is the value negative. What does that tell you?
2. **COMPUTE** a new variable, **HEATHGDP**, that calculates health expenditures per capita (**WDI_HE**) as a proportion of GDP per capita (**WDI_GDP**). The values should range from .03 to .24. The value for the United States is .20.

3.3 IF

Function: creates a new variable or revises an older one based upon some logical condition. An IF can be used to create a new variable from several others as with a **COMPUTE**.

IF (conditional expression is met) new variable=value.
. . . repeat for all categories of new variable.

Example 3.11—to create a new variable (**MINORITY**) to determine whether Blacks or Hispanics constitute the larger minority in a district (**CONGRESS2008**).

IF (BLACK > HISPANIC) MINORITY = 1.
IF (BLACK = HISPANIC) MINORITY = 2.
IF (BLACK < HISPANIC) MINORITY = 3.

The new values would be (1 = Black as predominant minority)(2 = equal) (3 = Hispanics).

FREQUENCIES VARIABLES=MINORITY.

MINORITY

		Frequency	Percent	Valid Percent	Cumulative Percent
Valid	1.00	203	46.7	46.7	46.7
	2.00	2	.5	.5	47.1
	3.00	230	52.9	52.9	100.0
	Total	435	100.0	100.0	

Caution:

As presented in this data file, **BLACK** and **HISPANIC** are not mutually exclusive categories.

Note: If any cases are excluded from any of the logical expressions (**IF**), the resulting variable, if it is new, will be assigned a missing value (**SYSMIS**) and will not be used in any future analysis that uses *that* variable.

Note: All logical expressions are possible, either in mathematical code or abbreviations:

$$<\qquad>\qquad<=\qquad>=\qquad=\qquad\neq$$

$$\text{LT}\qquad\text{GT}\qquad\text{LE}\qquad\text{GE}\qquad\text{EQ}\qquad\text{NE}$$

The new variable, **MINORITY**, could also have been created with a **COMPUTE (BLACK-HISPANIC)** and **RECODE** command (recoding all negative values together, etc.). In the **CONGRESS2008** data file, both variables are carried out to one decimal place.

COMPUTE MINORITY=BLACK-HISPANIC.
RECODE MINORITY (lo thru-0.09=3)(0=2)(0.09 thru hi=1).

Alternatively, a slightly altered use of the **COMPUTE** menu could be employed:

Step 1: From any **SPSS** window, left-click on "**Transform**," slide your cursor down to the first entry, "**Compute Variable**," and left-click it.

Step 2: Type the new variable name "**MINORITY**" into the "**Target Variable**" field. Create the first numeric expression by typing in the number "1" in that field.

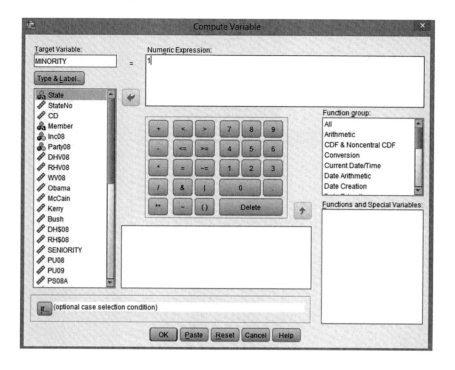

At this point, all districts will be coded as 1.

Step 3: Left-click on the "**If**" button. The following screen should appear:

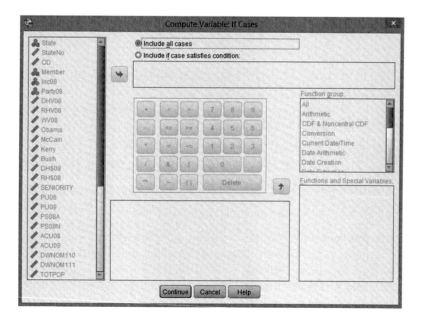

Step 4: Left-click on the second button, "**Include if case satisfies condition**." The field right below it should turn white.

Step 5: Using the same instructions as for **COMPUTE**, create the following logical expression in that white area: **BLACK > HISPANIC**.

Step 6: Left-click "**Continue**."

Step 7: Left-click "**OK**."

Repeat Steps 1 through 7 for the next two listed conditions.

After Step 7 ("**OK**") you will be asked if you want to change the existing variable. Left-click "**OK**." This is not as daunting as it may seem. You will notice that, at each new set, all of the remaining instructions are maintained. You just need to change the number in the "**numeric expression**" field (from 1 to 2 than to 3) and the operator within the **IF** dialog box (from **>** to **=** to **<**). Note that, as with the **RECODE** GUI, these transformational commands will remain if you use the IF command again.

IF: Sample Exercises

Follow any logical manipulation with a simple **FREQUENCIES** procedure of your new variable created by your **IF** statements in order to see your results:

FREQUENCIES VARIABLES=variable selected.

ANES2012A

For this exercise, weight the sample by **PW2012**.

Create a new variable, **IDEODIFF2,** that contains the following three categories about ideological placement:

Liberals>Conservatives (V75>V76)
Liberals=Conservatives (V75=V76)
Liberals<Conservatives (V75<V76)

Produce a frequency table for **IDEODIFF2**, along with the mode.

Congress2008–2012

The **COMPUTE** commands produced a measure of mean difference. We will now use the **IF** command to measure the number of districts where Democrats outspent Republicans or were outspent by Republicans (we have no ties but we'll enter in that possibility). Name that variable **DEME08 or DEME10 or DEME12**.

DHE>RHE (e.g., DHE08>RHE08)
DHE=RHE
DHE<RHE

Produce a frequency table for **DEM#(year)**, along with the mode.

EURO69

For each exercise, weight the sample by **W27**. If analyzing only one country or comparing just two countries against each other, use **W1**.

Create a new variable, **VOICEDIFF** that contains the following three categories about voice in one's **COUNTRY** versus the **EU**. Make sure to use the recoded versions of the variables that eliminated Don't Know (**DK**) responses (**RECODE**, exercise 4):

COUNTRY>EU (V12>V11)
COUNTRY=EU (V12=V11)
COUNTRY<EU (V12<V11)

Produce a frequency table for **VOICEDIFF**, along with the mode. Could we have produced the same results by computing the difference between the two variables? Why or why not?

CCES2012

For each exercise, weight the sample by **WEIGHT**.

Create a new variable, **PROXIMITY2,** that contains the following three categories about ideological placement:

ODIFF>RDIFF
ODIFF=RDIFF
ODIFF<RDIFF

How does **PROXIMITY2** match with **PROXIMITY?**

CROSSNAT

1. Return to our infant mortality example. Create a new variable **IMDIFF2** with three possible categories:

   WDI_IMM>WDI_IMF
   WDI_IMM=WDI_IMF
   WDI_IMM<WDI_IMF

   Notice anything unusual?

2. Create a new variable, **VOTEDIFF**, that compares presidential with parliamentary turnout with three possible categories:

IDEA_VTVAP_PA > IDEA_VTR_PR
IDEA_VTVAP_PA = IDEA_VTR_PR
IDEA_VTVAP_PA < IDEA_VTR_PR

Voter turnout in parliamentary elections will exceed turnout in presidential elections in an overwhelming majority of countries. Question: Why are there so many missing cases?

3.4 SELECT IF

Function: selects only a subset of the data for analysis.

SELECT IF (variable meets a certain logical condition).

Example 3.12—To select only individuals in the Eurobarometer survey living in countries with proportional representation systems (assuming the variable **ETYPE** was already created with a **RECODE**—see p. 23).

SELECT IF (ETYPE EQ 1).

SELECT IF can be used to analyze subgroups distinct from each other when combined with the **TEMPORARY** command. The **TEMPORARY** command will allow all data transformation procedures (e.g., **RECODE, SELECT IF**) to apply only until the first analytical procedure is performed. You then are returned to all of the original cases.

Note: some older versions of **SPSS** allow *SELECT IF to substitute for the two commands, **TEMPORARY** and **SELECT IF**. In the newer versions, anything preceded by an * is treated as an explanatory comment and just listed in your output.

Many analytical procedures will have a form of **TEMPORARY** and **SELECT IF** built in. See the discussion of controls in the **CROSSTABS** selection as an example (pp. 89–90).

To use the **GUI** menu to select only certain cases, perform the following steps.

Step 1: Left-click on "**Data**," move down to "**Select Cases**." The following dialog box should appear (if you have changed the options to "**Display names**"):

Step 2: Left-click on the circle next to "**If condition is satisfied**." Left-click on "**If**."

Step 3: In the open white field, create your logical statement (**ETYPE = 1**) much as you did with **COMPUTE** and **IF**. When completed, left-click "**Continue**."

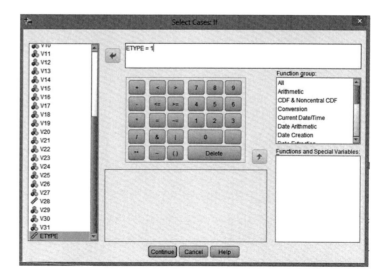

The dialog box in Step 1 will reappear, but with "**ETYPE = 1**" next to the "**If**" button. Left-click "**OK**."

Note: If you then repeat Steps 1 and 2 to select **ETYPE = 2**, you would logically expect that no cases would be left. Fortunately, in **GUI** mode, **SPSS** automatically resets the data spreadsheet to include all cases before performing the new **SELECT IF**. This is the equivalent of the **TEMPORARY** then **SELECT IF** set of syntax commands.

If you just want to return all cases to your active data spreadsheet, just go back to Step 1 and choose *"All cases."*

SELECT IF: Sample Exercises

Follow any **SELECT IF** with a simple **FREQUENCIES** procedure of the variable in order to see your selected results:

FREQUENCIES VARIABLES=variable selected.

ANES2012A

For each exercise, weight the sample by **PW2012**.

Choose any of the **RECODES, COMPUTES,** or **IF** procedures above, but produce the results only for those who voted in 2012 (**V64=2**).

Congress2008–2012

Choose any of the **RECODES, COMPUTES,** or **IF** procedures for this data set above, but produce the results only for open seats.

EURO69

Choose any of the **RECODES, COMPUTES,** or **IF** procedures above, but produce the results only for those individual residing in Spain and, separately, Portugal. As you are dealing with separate countries, make sure that you use

WEIGHT variable **W1** (not **W27**) before producing a **FREQUENCIES** for your variable(s).

For this exercise, you will need to precede each **SELECT IF** with a **TEMPORARY** command (see p. 23) before selecting your next country:

> **TEMPORARY.**
> **SELECT IF (COUNTRY EQ 6).**
> **. . . transformations and FREQUENCIES**
> **TEMPORARY.**
> **SELECT IF (COUNTRY EQ 14)**
> **. . . transformations and FREQUENCIES.**

For example, the first category of your recoded **V20A** (Globalization-Threat to National Culture) should contain 33.7% of the cases in Spain and 47.3% of the cases in Portugal.

CCES2012

For each exercise, weight the sample by **WEIGHT**.

1. Choose any of the **RECODES, COMPUTES,** or **IF** procedures above, but produce the results only for those without health insurance (**V20=2**). Note any differences.
2. Choose the three previously Recoded Party ID variables. Temporarily select only respondents from California (**STATE=6**). Produce frequency distributions for those three variables. Next, temporarily select only respondents from Texas (**STATE=48**). Produce the same three frequencies. What can you say about the differences between Californians and Texans?

CROSSNAT

Choose any of the **RECODES, COMPUTES,** or **IF** procedures for this data set above, but produce the results only for countries with a proportional electoral system (**IDEA_ESF=1**).

CONTENTS

Commonly Used SPSS Commands— Data Analysis

Once all appropriate transformations have been done, you will then proceed to analyzing the data in order to confirm or disconfirm your hypotheses. Several types of statistical analysis are possible. Four will be presented here. Examples will be given for each, along with an explanation of the output that **SPSS** will produce. For each of these sets of analysis, the **GUI** interface always starts with left-clicking on the "Analyze" tab.

▌ 4.1 FREQUENCIES

Function: creates a frequency distribution of each specified variable and, if asked for, statistics to go along with that distribution. It is recommended that frequencies be produced for all variables on which you wish to perform a **RECODE**, especially in the **ANES2008A** file. That will allow you to check out whether you should employ the "conceptual" or "practical" model of reclassifying information. Once recoded, you can also use **FREQUENCIES** to make sure that the recode was done correctly.

For more on this topic, see Chapter 2 (for distributions and graphs) and Chapters 3 and 4 (for statistics) in *Understanding Political Science Statistics: Observations and Expectations in Political Analysis*.

FREQUENCIES VARIABLES = variable or variable list.

Example 4.1—To view a distribution of the party identification measure (**V36**) in the **ANES2008A** file.

FREQUENCIES VARIABLES = V36.

With no further instructions, the following will be produced (remember, you would first need to **GET** the file, and **WEIGHT** it). In all examples, the **ANES** weight **PW2** was used. Note that no summary statistics are provided. Also note that **SPSS** will produce cumulative frequencies even if the data are not ordinal. The program has no way of knowing that, but you would know not to interpret it.

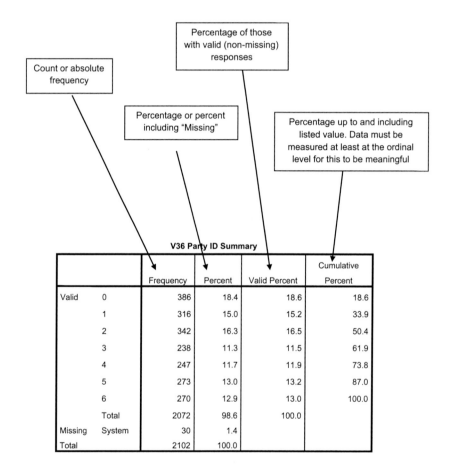

V36 Party ID Summary

		Frequency	Percent	Valid Percent	Cumulative Percent
Valid	0	386	18.4	18.6	18.6
	1	316	15.0	15.2	33.9
	2	342	16.3	16.5	50.4
	3	238	11.3	11.5	61.9
	4	247	11.7	11.9	73.8
	5	273	13.0	13.2	87.0
	6	270	12.9	13.0	100.0
	Total	2072	98.6	100.0	
Missing	System	30	1.4		
Total		2102	100.0		

To use the **GUI** interface, (1) left-click on the "**Analyze**" tab, then (2) move down to "**Descriptive Statistics**," and (3) slide over to and left-click "**Frequencies**":

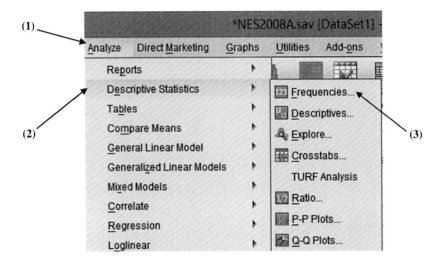

The following dialog box will appear (it may be stretched out horizontally):

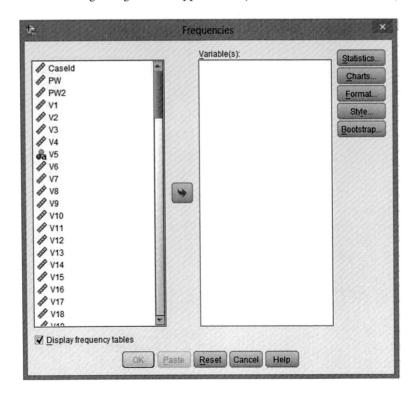

Step 4: Move the cursor down to **V36** (Party ID Summary) and drag, double click, or left-click on the arrow button. You can include as many variables as you wish:

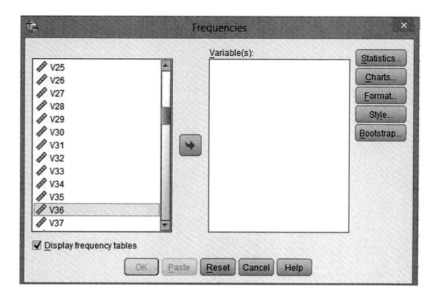

V36 will now appear in your "**Variable(s)**" field. If you left-click on the "**OK**" button, you will get a summary of the statistic (Valid and Missing N) and the frequency listing shown below.

Example 4.2—To view a distribution of the party identification measure (**V36**) in the **ANES2008A** file and compute relevant statistics. **Mode** and **Median** would be useful here. Frequency table would appear as below.

FREQUENCIES VARIABLES = V36/STATISTICS=MODE MEDIAN.

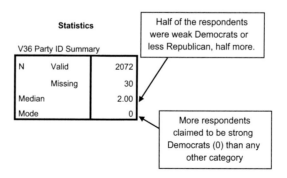

Statistics

V36 Party ID Summary

N	Valid	2072
	Missing	30
Median		2.00
Mode		0

Half of the respondents were weak Democrats or less Republican, half more.

More respondents claimed to be strong Democrats (0) than any other category

Caution:

If more than one mode exits, **SPSS** will only present the first. Look at the frequency distribution to make sure.

Example 4.3—**FREQUENCIES** (as well as **DESCRIPTIVES**) will produce a host of statistics, but they're not very useful unless you have data measured at the interval level. You can produce these statistics without the long listing of values. Let's turn to the **CONGRESS2008** file, variable **COLLEGE**. The **FORMAT=NOTABLE** suppresses what would be a very long table:

FREQUENCIES VARIABLES = COLLEGE/STATISTICS = ALL /FORMAT = NOTABLE.

The following will be produced. Some of the statistics are interpreted for you.

Statistics

COLLEGE

N	Valid	435
	Missing	0
Mean		26.728736
Std. Error of Mean		.4583380
Median		25.000000
Mode		19.3000
Std. Deviation		9.5593960
Variance		91.382
Skewness		.888
Std. Error of Skewness		.117
Kurtosis		.786
Std. Error of Kurtosis		.234
Range		56.1000
Minimum		6.7000
Maximum		62.8000
Sum		11627.0000

In 50% of the districts, the percentage of college grads was 25% or less, in 50% the percentage is 50% or more.

The percentage of college grads in each district does not vary by more than 56.1% (Maximum-Minimum).

Note: As mentioned in the first part of the **SPSS** guide, you can produce multiple frequencies with or without statistics and with or without tables. Just list the variables separated by a comma and/or space. For example, to produce statistics for both **COLLEGE** and **MEDIANAGE**:

FREQUENCIES VARIABLES = COLLEGE, MEDIANAGE /STATISTICS = ALL/FORMAT = NOTABLE.

Example 4.4—To produce the median and mean for our newly computed variables **IDEODIFF** and **RACEDIFF** (see **RECODE** examples 4.7 and 4.8, **ANES2008A**), suppressing what would be very long frequency tables:

COMPUTE IDEODIFF = V75-V76.
COMPUTE RACEDIFF = V80-V78.
FREQUENCIES VARIABLES=IDEODIFF, RACEDIFF
  /FORMAT=NOTABLE/STATISTICS=MEDIAN MEAN.

Statistics

		IDEODIFF	RACEDIFF
N	Valid	1979	2044
	Missing	123	58
Mean		-5.6429	4.1698
Median		.0000	.0000

Note that fewer sampled individuals answered both ideological questions (**V75** and/or **V76**) than did race questions (**V80** and/or **V78**). Question: What does a median of 0 degrees tell you?

Example 4.5—To produce the median and mean for our newly computed **SPENDDIFF** variable (see **RECODE** example 4.8, **CONGRESS2008**):

COMPUTE SPENDDIFF=RHE08—DHE08.
FREQUENCIES VARIABLES=SPENDDIFF/FORMAT=NOTABLE
  /STATISTICS=MEDIAN MEAN.

Statistics

SPENDDIFF

N	Valid	435
	Missing	0
Mean		-169892.7195
Median		-469959.0000

Note: The following statistics can be chosen separately if one doesn't want all (**STATISTICS=ALL**) of them listed (see Chapters 3–4 of text for discussion of many of these):

MEAN   STDDEV   VARIANCE   RANGE   MINIMUM   MAXIMUM   SEMEAN

MEDIAN   MODE   SUM   SKEWNESS   SESKEW   KURTOSIS   SEKURT

Example 4.6—To produce basic charts for a frequency distribution. Let's turn back to our frequency distribution of partisan identification. To produce a bar chart of the seven identification categories (suppressing the tables):

FREQUENCIES VARIABLES = V36/BARCHART PERCENT
/FORMAT=NOTABLE.

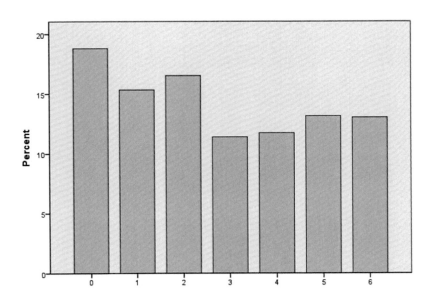

Cases weighted by WT.2. CROSS-SECTION SAMPLE WEIGHT - POST-ELECTION: centered

One could also produce a histogram (bars together with statistics) or pie chart by substituting either **HISTOGRAM** or **PIE** for **BARCHART**.

All of the statistics, charts, etc., can be produced using the **GUI** interface and appropriate dialogue boxes. For example, to suppress tables*, one would (1) uncheck the "**Display frequencies tables**" button. To choose Statistics, one would (2) left-click on the "**Statistics**" button. To create a basic chart, one would (3) left-click on the "**Charts**" button:

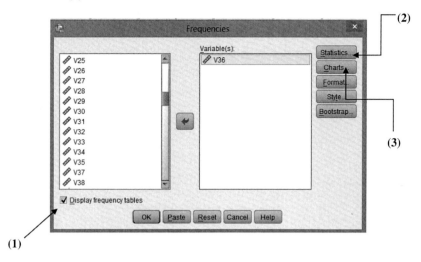

For step 2, the following dialog box will appear. Choose your statistics by left-clicking on the appropriate button(s) and left-clicking the "**Continue**" button:

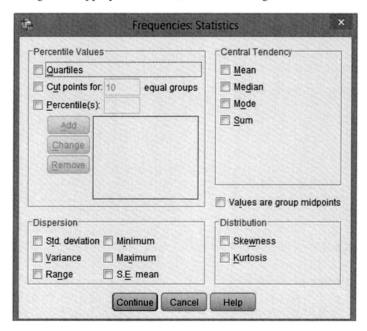

*Note: The **DESCRIPTIVES** procedure will also produce *most* statistics without a frequency distribution table. It will not, however, allow you to produce charts, nor compute a median.

Note that, just as with the original listing of cumulative frequencies, **SPSS** will not deny you the opportunity to choose statistics that are not appropriate for your level of measurement. It will calculate a mean of a listing of, for example the four Census categories even though that mean is, well, meaningless.

For step 3, the following dialogue box will appear. Choose your chart type by left-clicking on the appropriate button and then left-clicking on the "**Continue**" button. You can choose to have either raw **Frequencies** or **Percentages** shown on **Bar** and **Pie** (but not **Histograms**) charts:

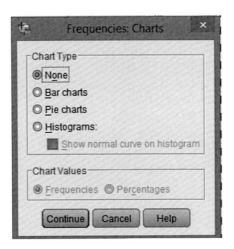

When you have completed either or both dialogue boxes, you will be returned to the original frequency box. Left-click "**OK**" to carry out the full frequency procedure.

FREQUENCIES: Sample Exercises

You should already have enough practice with the items above, but you may also try the following.

ANES2012A

For each exercise, weight the sample by **PW2012**.

1. Produce a **BARCHART** for **PRESAPPROVE**, computed above. What can you say about President Obama's job approval?
2. Produce a **BARCHART** and **PIECHART** of **IDEODIFF**. What can you say about Americans' ideological preferences?
3. Repeat #2, but only for voters (**SELECT IF**). Any difference?

Congress2008–2012

1. Produce a **PIECHART** for each of the winning party variables (**PARTY08. PARTY10, PARTY12**). What has changed over time?
2. Produce a **BARCHART** and **PIECHART** for the original Incumbency Status Variables (**INC08, INC10, INC12**).

EURO69

For each exercise, weight the sample by **W27**. If analyzing only one country or comparing just two countries against each other, use W1.

1. Produce a **BARCHART** for **EUVOICE**, computed in **COMPUTE** exercise 2. What can you say about one's perception of one's voice counting in the EU and one's Country?
2. Produce a **BARCHART** and **PIECHART** of **V20A**.
3. Repeat step 2, but only for men (**SELECT IF**). Any difference?

CCES2012

For each exercise, weight the sample by **WEIGHT**.

1. Produce a **BARCHART** for **PROXIMITY**, computed above. What can you say about one's ideological proximity to the two major party candidates?
2. Produce a **PIECHART** for your three previously recoded Party ID variables. What can you say about Americans' partisan preferences in 2012?
3. Using frequency distributions and BARCHARTs, compare adult American's views towards tax cuts and deficits (**V43, V43, V45**).

CROSSNAT

1. To demonstrate the extreme difference in infant mortality rates for males and females, produce a **PIECHART** for **IMDIFF2** (**COMPUTE** exercise 1).
2. PRODUCE BARCHARTs for every variable dealing with funding and subsidies for elections: **IDEA_DPFP** to **IDEA_LCS**. Where does the difference seem greatest? The bar heights seem to reverse. Does this signify a change in electoral policy direction or a difference in the variable coding?
3. Produce a **HISTOGRAM** for your previously computed **HEALTHGDP** (**COMPUTE** exercise 2). Describe the shape and skew of the distribution.

4.2 MEANS*

Function: Compute means and other statistics of one variable for each category of a second variable (again, as with a controlled crosstab, make sure that you do not have too many categories).

For more on this topic, see Chapters 3–5 in *Understanding Political Science Statistics: Observations and Expectations in Political Analysis.*

MEANS TABLES=variable(s) for which statistics are generated
  by variable from which categories will be separated
  /CELLS = list of statistics.

Example 4.7—Compute means, medians, standard deviation, and range of feeling thermometer scores for Sarah Palin (**ANES2008A, variable = V72**) for men and, separately, women (**V1**) and give the number of valid responses (**COUNT = N**) for each.

MEANS TABLES=V72 by V1
  /CELLS=MEAN MEDIAN STDDEV RANGE COUNT.

---

*For much older versions of SPSS, the MEANS procedure does not exist. The following would, however, produce the same results.
 Older SPSS

  TEMPORARY.
  SELECT IF (V1 EQ 1).
  FREQUENCIES VARIABLES=V72
   /STATISTICS=MEAN MEDIAN STDDEV RANGE.
  TEMPORARY.
  SELECT IF (V1 EQ 2).
  FREQUENCIES VARIABLES=V72
   /STATISTICS=MEAN MEDIAN STDDEV RANGE.

Example 4.8—Produce the same statistics for the **ACU** scores given to Democratic (**PARTY=1**) and Republican (**PARTY=2**) members of the U.S. House (**CONGRESS2008.SAV**) who ran for reelection in 2008 and for all elected members in 2009.

Mean, median, standard deviation, range, and N (COUNT or number of cases) for the 967 responding men (V1=1).

WEIGHT=PW2

Report

D1u. Feeling thermometer: SARAH PALIN

HHList.1. Respondent: gender	Mean	Median	Std. Deviation	Range	N
1	51.50	50.00	26.728	100	967
2	51.13	50.00	28.086	100	1054
Total	51.31	50.00	27.439	100	2020

Mean, median, standard deviation, range, and N (COUNT or number of cases) for the 1054 responding women (V1=2).

MEANS TABLES=ACU08 ACU09 by PARTY
/CELLS=MEAN MEDIAN STDDEV RANGE COUNT.

Report

Party		ACU08	ACU09
1	Mean	6.64	6.77
	Median	4.00	.00
	Std. Deviation	7.837	11.249
	Range	41	72
	N	222	255
2	Mean	84.89	91.28
	Median	90.00	96.00
	Std. Deviation	16.390	10.245
	Range	72	45
	N	155	177
Total	Mean	38.81	41.39
	Median	13.00	16.50
	Std. Deviation	40.406	42.996
	Range	100	100
	N	377	432

Exercise: Compare the statistics for Democrats and Republicans and all members for either 2008 or 2009.

Compare the statistics between 2008 and 2009. Remember, however, that ACU08 scores only exist for those who ran for reelection, so the number of cases is different. What might that tell you about the new members of Congress?

To use the **GUI** interface for Means, (1) left-click on the "**Analyze**" tab, then (2) move down to "**Compare Means**" and (3) slide over and left-click "**Means**":

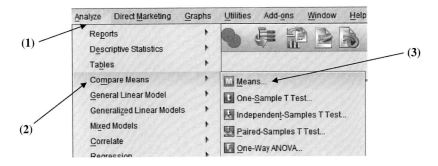

The following will appear:

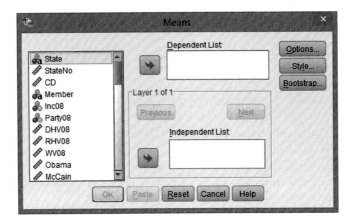

Using any of the methods discussed previously, move **ACU08**, the **ACU09** into the "**Dependent List**" frame. Move **Party08** into the "**Independent List**" frame. If you Left-click "**OK**," only the default statistics (**Mean**, **Number of Cases (Count)**, **Standard Deviation**) will appear in the output table. If you want to calculate more statistics, you must, before left-clicking **OK**, left-click on "**Options. . .**". Move over any other needed statistics and then left-click "**Continue**." Then, from the original **Means** dialog box, left-click "**OK**."

MEANS: Sample Exercises

ANES2012A

For each exercise, weight the sample by **PW2012**.

1. Using the feeling thermometer rating for former President George W. Bush (**V15**), compute and interpret the means and standard deviations for men and women (**V1**).
2. Do the same for feeling thermometer ratings of President Obama (**V16**) and former Governor W. Mitt Romney (**V17**). Discuss the differences and similarities among the three.

Congress2008–2012

1. Using the percentage of black residents in a district for any year (**BLACK08 or BLACK 10 or BLACK 12**), compute and interpret the means and standard deviations for districts won by Democrats and districts won by Republicans (use the matching **PARTY08 or PARTY10 or PARTY12**).
2. Do the same for per capita income (**PCI08 or PCI10 or PCI12**).

EURO69

For each exercise, weight the sample by **W27**. If analyzing only one country or comparing just two countries against each other, use **W1**.

1. Using the intention to vote scale (**V22**) compute and interpret the means and standard deviations for men and women (**V27**).
2. Do the same for each of the three categories of your computed variable **EUVOICE**. On mean average, which **EUVOICE** group is most/least likely to intend to vote?

CCES2012

For each exercise, weight the sample by **WEIGHT**.

1. Using the percentage allocation for budget deficits (**V60**), produce means, medians, and standard deviations for those who voted for Obama, Romney, and any other candidate. Discuss the differences.
2. Do the same for (**V60**) for your three previously created (**IF**) categories of **PROXIMITY2**. Discuss the differences and compare your findings to exercise ANES2012A.

Note that in both, we are comparing *profiles* of Obama and Romney supporters/proximates. The actual *causal order* (are you more likely to vote for a candidate based on how you feel about budget deficits or for the candidate you are more ideologically proximate to?) is not presented in profiles.

CROSSNAT

1. Using the **MEANS** procedure, does compulsory voting seem to increase voting turnout for parliament and, separately, for president? Use the voting age population figures for each.
2. We know that voting turnout in the United States is higher during presidential election years than non-presidential years, leading to the conclusion that presidential elections are viewed as more salient and exciting. As an indirect follow-up test to this hypothesis, is turnout for parliamentary elections, on mean average, higher in countries with a president than those without? Use your previously recoded variable **IDEA_ESP** that separated countries into those with presidential election systems and those without.

4.3 T-TEST

Function: Performs several comparisons of means tests. One can use **T-TEST** to (1) determine if the mean of a certain variable is significantly different from a hypothesized mean or the probable range of the mean of the population from which a sample was randomly drawn. One can also (2) compare the mean values of two different variables within a data set (in order to determine if they are significantly different from each other) or (3) compare and test for significance the difference of one variable on two different groups within a sample.

For more on this topic, see Chapters 5–7 in *Understanding Political Science Statistics: Observations and Expectations in Political Analysis.*

Form 1: One Sample, One or More Variables Tested against a Hypothesized Population Value

T-TEST TESTVAL = test value/VARIABLES = variable(s).

Example 4.9—To test whether the mean support for Sarah Palin (**ANES2008A**) is significantly different from 50 (neutral). The **WEIGHT** was set to **PW2**.

T-TEST TESTVAL = 50/VARIABLES = V72.

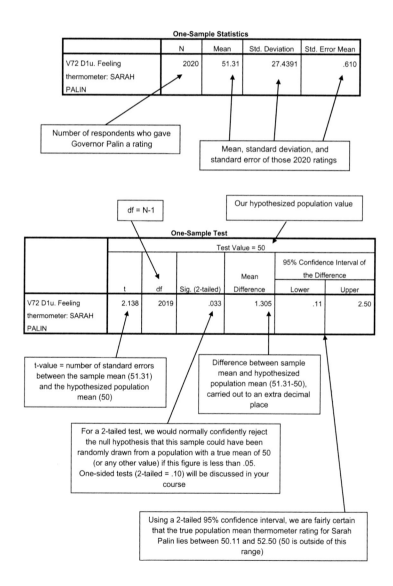

One-Sample Statistics

	N	Mean	Std. Deviation	Std. Error Mean
V72 D1u. Feeling thermometer: SARAH PALIN	2020	51.31	27.4391	.610

Number of respondents who gave Governor Palin a rating

Mean, standard deviation, and standard error of those 2020 ratings

df = N-1

Our hypothesized population value

One-Sample Test

	Test Value = 50					
					95% Confidence Interval of the Difference	
	t	df	Sig. (2-tailed)	Mean Difference	Lower	Upper
V72 D1u. Feeling thermometer: SARAH PALIN	2.138	2019	.033	1.305	.11	2.50

t-value = number of standard errors between the sample mean (51.31) and the hypothesized population mean (50)

Difference between sample mean and hypothesized population mean (51.31-50), carried out to an extra decimal place

For a 2-tailed test, we would normally confidently reject the null hypothesis that this sample could have been randomly drawn from a population with a true mean of 50 (or any other value) if this figure is less than .05. One-sided tests (2-tailed = .10) will be discussed in your course

Using a 2-tailed 95% confidence interval, we are fairly certain that the true population mean thermometer rating for Sarah Palin lies between 50.11 and 52.50 (50 is outside of this range)

To produce this output using the **GUI** interface, (1) left-click on "**Analyze**," (2) slide down to "**Compare Means**," and then (3) slide over to and left-click "**One-Sample T-Test**."

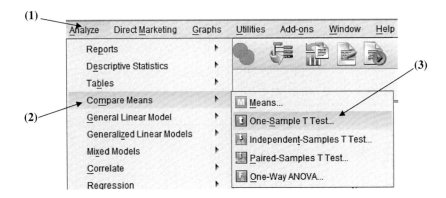

The following will appear:

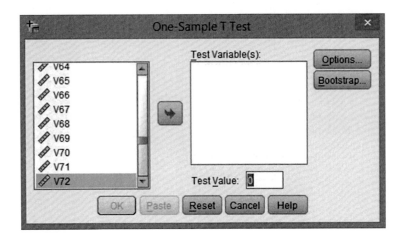

Move down and move **V72** (feeling thermometer—Sarah Palin) into the "**Test Variable(s)**" field. Type "50" into the "**Test Value**" field. Left-click "**OK**." The above output should be produced.

Form 2: One Sample, Two Variables (Paired Samples— "Dependent" Test)

T-TEST PAIRS = variable(s) WITH variable(s).

Example 4.10—To test whether the mean support for Sarah Palin (**V72**) is significantly different from the mean support for Joe Biden (**V71**).

T-TEST PAIRS = V72 with V71.

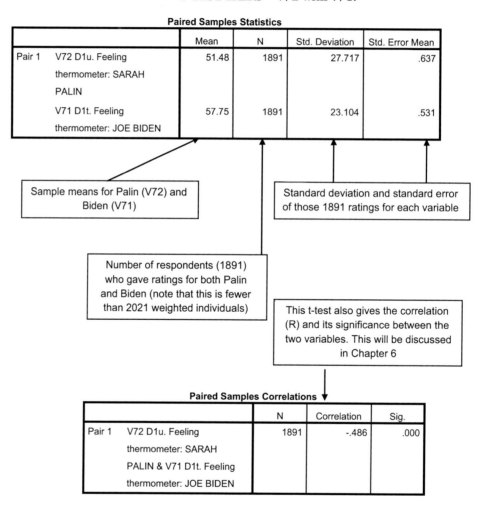

Paired Samples Statistics

		Mean	N	Std. Deviation	Std. Error Mean
Pair 1	V72 D1u. Feeling thermometer: SARAH PALIN	51.48	1891	27.717	.637
	V71 D1t. Feeling thermometer: JOE BIDEN	57.75	1891	23.104	.531

Sample means for Palin (V72) and Biden (V71)

Standard deviation and standard error of those 1891 ratings for each variable

Number of respondents (1891) who gave ratings for both Palin and Biden (note that this is fewer than 2021 weighted individuals)

This t-test also gives the correlation (R) and its significance between the two variables. This will be discussed in Chapter 6

Paired Samples Correlations

		N	Correlation	Sig.
Pair 1	V72 D1u. Feeling thermometer: SARAH PALIN & V71 D1t. Feeling thermometer: JOE BIDEN	1891	-.486	.000

Note: Tables may be truncated after they are exported into Word with some redundancy. Alternatively, as will be shown later, one can export the table to fit within the margins of your Word page as below.

Paired Samples Test

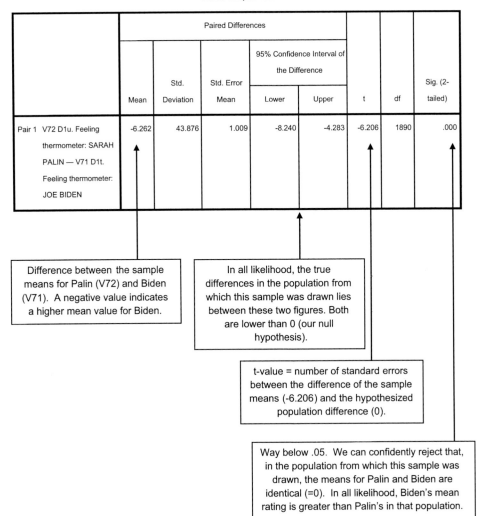

	Paired Differences							
				95% Confidence Interval of the Difference				Sig. (2-tailed)
	Mean	Std. Deviation	Std. Error Mean	Lower	Upper	t	df	
Pair 1 V72 D1u. Feeling thermometer: SARAH PALIN — V71 D1t. Feeling thermometer: JOE BIDEN	-6.262	43.876	1.009	-8.240	-4.283	-6.206	1890	.000

Difference between the sample means for Palin (V72) and Biden (V71). A negative value indicates a higher mean value for Biden.

In all likelihood, the true differences in the population from which this sample was drawn lies between these two figures. Both are lower than 0 (our null hypothesis).

t-value = number of standard errors between the difference of the sample means (-6.206) and the hypothesized population difference (0).

Way below .05. We can confidently reject that, in the population from which this sample was drawn, the means for Palin and Biden are identical (=0). In all likelihood, Biden's mean rating is greater than Palin's in that population.

Note: A "significant difference" doesn't necessarily mean that your hypothesis is correct. What if you hypothesized that the mean thermometer rating for Palin was *greater* than Biden's? Or, for the first example, what if you hypothesized that, for the entire sample, it was *less* than 50? The differences are significant, but in our examples they are in the *wrong* direction. The same "directional" rule for hypotheses will apply in our other statistics to follow.

To produce this output using the **GUI** interface, (1) left-click on "**Analyze**," (2) slide down to "**Compare Means**," and then (3) slide over to and left-click "**Paired-Samples T-Test**":

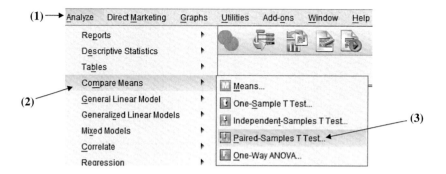

The following will appear:

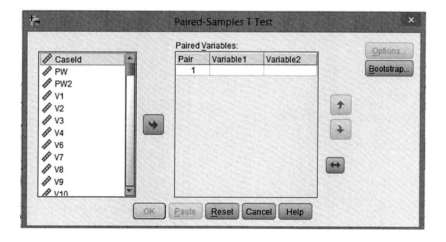

Move down and select **V72** and move it into the space below "**Variable1**." Move **V71** into the space below "**Variable2**." Left-click "**OK**" and the above output should be produced. You will note that once the first variable is moved over, a second row (Pair-2) will show up. This allows you to compare any combination of the means of variables. The "**Options**" feature allows you to set the confidence interval (defaults at 95% two-tailed) and how you want missing cases treated. The default is to exclude those who didn't give a listed response to either of the two variables in each pairing. If you are running a series of comparisons, you will be allowed to exclude anyone who is missing on any of the variables selected (so as to be able to compare the same individuals across all comparisons).

Form 3: One or More Variables, Two Different Subsamples ("Independent Samples Test")

T-TEST GROUPS = grouping variable (group value 1, group value 2) /VARIABLES=variable(s) for which means are requested.

Example 4.11—To test whether the mean support for Sarah Palin (**V72**) is significantly different between men and women (categories 1 and 2 on **V1**, respectively).

T-TEST GROUPS = V1 (1, 2)/ VARIABLES = V72.

Note: The "group values" are whatever they are in the codebook. The values specified in this example (1, 2) are specific only for V1. If we wanted to compare the differences between those who voted for Obama and those who voted for McCain, the values would be (1, 3).

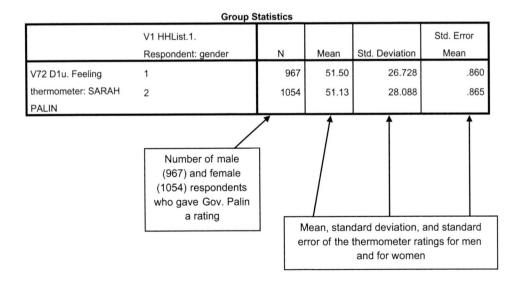

Group Statistics

	V1 HHList.1. Respondent: gender	N	Mean	Std. Deviation	Std. Error Mean
V72 D1u. Feeling thermometer: SARAH PALIN	1	967	51.50	26.728	.860
	2	1054	51.13	28.088	.865

Number of male (967) and female (1054) respondents who gave Gov. Palin a rating

Mean, standard deviation, and standard error of the thermometer ratings for men and for women

For this part of the table, I had MS Word rotate some of the labeling to fit the reduced table size (exported to fit the page).

Independent Samples Test

		Levene's Test for Equality of Variances		t-test for Equality of Means						95% Confidence Interval of the Difference	
		F	Sig.	t	df	Sig. (2-tailed)	Mean Difference	Std. Error Difference		Lower	Upper
V72 D1u. Feeling thermometer: SARAH PALIN	Equal variances assumed	4.934	.026	.300	2018	.764	.367	1.222		-2.030	2.764
	Equal variances not assumed			.301	2015.717	.764	.367	1.220		-2.025	2.759

If the significance of "F" is greater than .05, then we assume equal variances, otherwise we assume different variances in the two subsamples.
We assume unequal variances here. With large samples, the differences will not be dramatic (see rest of table).

Differences between male and female means in the sample (.367).

Significance is much greater than .05 (2-tailed). We can't confidently reject that, in the population from which this sample was drawn, the means for males and females are identical. The sample mean difference of .367 is not significantly different enough from 0.00.

In all likelihood, the true population differences between males and females are somewhere between -2.025 and +2.759. The value of 0 is within this range and thus *cannot* be rejected as a possibility.

To produce this output using the **GUI** interface, (1) left-click on "**Analyze**," (2) slide down to "**Compare Means**," and then (3) slide over to and left-click "**Independent-Samples T-Test**":

(1)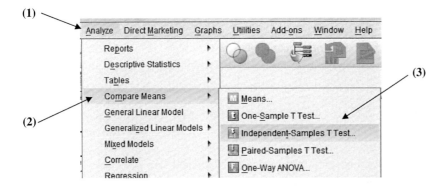

(2)

(3)

The following will appear:

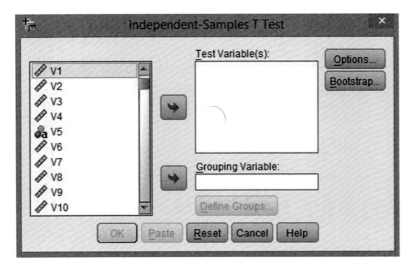

Move down the variable list, select **V72** and move it into the "**Test Variable(s)**" blank field. Move **V1** into the "**Grouping Variable**" field. The "**Define Groups …**" button will become active. Left click on that button:

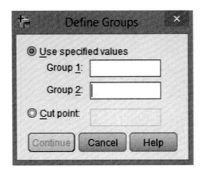

Two options exist. In the first, "**Use specified values**," you will type in the numbers corresponding to each of the two groups you want to compare the means of on your selected variable(s). For gender (**V1**) this is easy. The numbers are "1" and "2," corresponding to "male" and "female," respectively.

What if, however, we wanted to compare those who hoped the United States would have a woman president in his/her lifetime (**V90**, category 1) with those who didn't hope (**V90**, category 3) for a woman president? The relevant numbers to list for the two groups would then be "1" and "3."

The second option allows you to split ordered categories into two groupings, by left-clicking on the "**cut point**" button. Here are some possibilities (refer to **ANES2008** codebook):

Grouping variable	Cutoff	Two groups compared
V61 Education	4*	**Bachelors or higher (4,5)/**
		≤ HS (1,2,3)
V62 Household Income	14	**≥ $350000 / < $350000**
V76 FT—Conservatives	60	**≥ median / < median**

*The cutoff value will always be included in the first, higher category. Note that we could have accomplished the same goal by first recoding each of the variables into two categories, and then, using the first option, specifying "1" and "2" as our two specified values. A preliminary recode is most essential when no neat ordering exists in our original grouping variable. For example, what if we wanted to compare those who fit the "traditional" marriage categorization—married or widowed (**V60**, categories 1, 4) with all others?

Note: If you choose more than one variable to use to compare means (or most other statistical procedures), you may wind up with variables or comparisons with different numbers of cases. Some items are just answered by more respondents than others. You have two options:

1. Compare each against each other regardless of case numbers.
2. Only use those cases that have a listed response for all compared variables. This is called a "listwise" deletion.

For example, if you ran the following:

T-TEST GROUPS = V1 (1, 2)/VARIABLES = V71, V72.

You will produce (first part of output):

Group Statistics

	V1 HHList.1. Respondent: gender	N	Mean	Std. Deviation	Std. Error Mean
V71 D1t. Feeling thermometer: JOE BIDEN	1	932	54.97	23.235	.761
	2	979	60.57	22.617	.723
V72 D1u. Feeling thermometer: SARAH PALIN	1	967	51.50	26.728	.860
	2	1054	51.13	28.086	.865

Notice that more male (1) and female (2) respondents were able to rate Governor Sarah Palin than Senator Joseph Biden. To compare the two feeling thermometer breakdowns only for those who gave a response to both variables, add the following in syntax:

**T-TEST GROUPS = V1 (1, 2)/VARIABLES = V71, V72
/MISSING=LISTWISE.**

Group Statistics

	V1 HHList.1. Respondent: gender	N	Mean	Std. Deviation	Std. Error Mean
V71 D1t. Feeling thermometer: JOE BIDEN	1	918	54.85	23.293	.769
	2	973	60.48	22.600	.724
V72 D1u. Feeling thermometer: SARAH PALIN	1	918	51.69	26.994	.891
	2	973	51.29	28.396	.910

Not much of a change in outcomes, but this may not always be true, especially when the number of cases really vary.

The **GUI** version is rather straightforward and generally appears as an **OPTION**. On the main dialogue box for the independent samples t-test, left-click on the "**Options**" button. The following will appear. Click the "**Exclude cases listwise**" button.

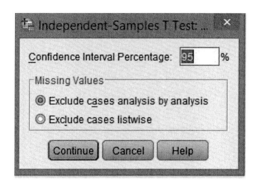

Sample Exercises

ANES2012A

For each exercise, weight the sample by **PW2012**.

1. Using the feeling thermometer rating for former President George W. Bush (**V15**), can you confidently reject ($p < .05$) the possibility that this sample, with a mean of 46 degrees, could have been randomly drawn from a population with a mean of 50 degrees or higher? Use the **T-TEST TESTVAL** format (Form 1). Your answer should be "**YES.**" Using 95% confidence interval testing procedures (see two-curve examples in text), what would you estimate the range of mean thermometer values to be in the population from which this sample was (randomly) drawn?

2. Can you confidently reject that it is no lower than 45 degrees? Your answer should be "**NO.**" Use the **T-TEST TESTVAL** procedure to confirm this.

3. Using the **T-TEST GROUPS** procedure (Form 3), is the difference between Latinos and non-Latinos (**V3**) on **V15** significant? That is, is the difference observed in the sample large enough to confidently reject the null hypothesis of no difference in the population? Your answer should be "**YES.**" Which group feels "warmer" toward George Bush on mean average?

4. Using the **T-TEST PAIRS** procedure (Form 2), is there a significant difference between the mean feeling thermometer rating of former President Bush (**V15**) and 2012 GOP candidate W. Mitt Romney (**V17**)? Your answer should be "**YES.**"

EURO69

For each exercise, weight the sample by **W27**. If analyzing only one country or comparing just two countries against each other, use W1.

1. Using the 10-point perception of global warming scale (**V24**), can you confidently reject ($p < .05$) the possibility that this sample, with a mean of 7.84 could have been randomly drawn from a population with a mean of 5.5 degrees (middle of the scale) or lower? Use the **T-TEST TESTVAL** format (Form 1). Your answer should be "**YES**." Using 95% confidence interval testing procedures (see two-curve examples in text), what would you estimate the range of mean perceptions to be in the population from which this sample was (randomly) drawn?

2. Can you confidently reject that it is no lower than an 7.75? Your answer should be "**YES**." Use the **T-TEST TESTVAL** procedure to confirm this. Why is such a small difference statistically significant?

3. For the following, you will compare only those who felt both their countries and their own voice counted in the EU (**EUVOICE=2**) with those who felt it counted in neither (**EU=4**). Using the **T-TEST GROUPS** procedure (Form 3), is the difference between those two groups' mean intention to vote (**V22**) significantly different? That is, is the difference observed in the sample large enough to confidently reject the null hypothesis of no difference in the population?

4. Using the **T-TEST GROUPS** procedure (Form 3), is the difference between males and females (**V27**) on **V22** significant? That is, is the difference observed in the sample large enough to confidently reject the null hypothesis of no difference in the population?

CCES2012

For each exercise, weight the sample by **WEIGHT**.

1. Using the percentage allocation for budget deficits (**V60**), can you confidently reject ($p < .05$) the possibility that this sample could have been randomly drawn from a population with a mean value equal to a 50/50 allocation split between tax increases and cuts? Use the **T-TEST TESTVAL** format (Form 1). Your answer should be "**YES**." Using 95% confidence interval testing procedures (see two-curve examples in text), what would you estimate the range of mean allocation values to be in the population from which this sample was (randomly) drawn?

2. Repeat step 1, but this time change your population estimate to 58% cuts. Can you still reject this null hypothesis? Your answer should still be "**YES**." Explain your findings. Why can such a small difference between what we observe in the sample and our population expectation be statistically significant?

4.4 NPAR: TESTS FOR PROPORTIONS

Function: These legacy non-parametric tests can be used for inferential tests for single variable proportions.

For more on this topic, see Chapter 8 in *Understanding Political Science Statistics: Observations and Expectations in Political Analysis.*

Form 1: Dichotomous Proportions

NPAR TESTS
/BINOMIAL (comparison proportion) = variable(s).

Example 4.12—To test whether the proportion who voted (**V64**, whether or not one voted in 2008) is significantly different than .50 (.50%) in the population from which this sample was (randomly) drawn.

NPAR TESTS/BINOMIAL (.50) = V64.

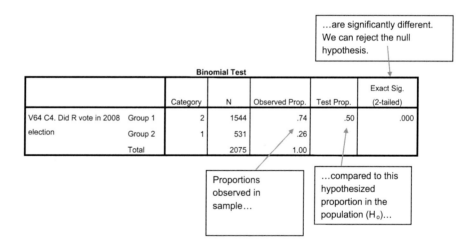

Binomial Test

		Category	N	Observed Prop.	Test Prop.	Exact Sig. (2-tailed)
V64 C4. Did R vote in 2008 election	Group 1	2	1544	.74	.50	.000
	Group 2	1	531	.26		
	Total		2075	1.00		

…are significantly different. We can reject the null hypothesis.

Proportions observed in sample…

…compared to this hypothesized proportion in the population (H_o)…

To produce this output using the **GUI** interface, (1) left-click on "**Analyze**," (2) slide down to "**Nonparametric Tests**," then (3) slide over to "**Legacy Dialogues**," and (4) left-click "**Binomial**":

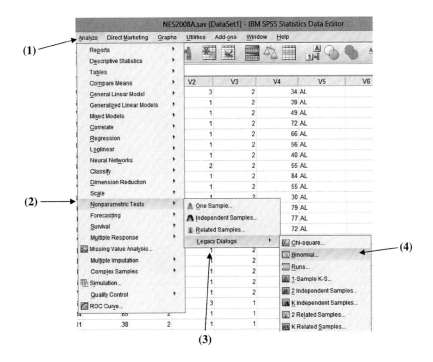

The following will appear:

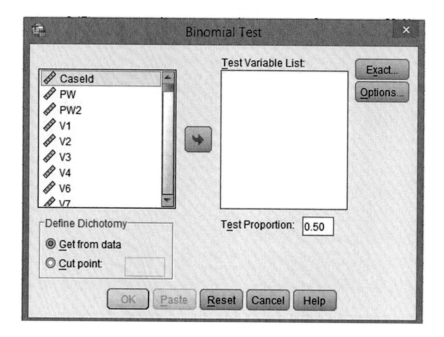

Move down the variable list, select **V64** and move it into the "**Test Variable List**" blank field. The default population proportion is .50. You can change that if you want to compare your sample against a different hypothesized population value. Left click on "**OK.**" Again, keep in mind that "significantly different" might be "significantly different" in the wrong direction. Reversing the number of voters and non-voters would produce the same results.

Form 2: Single Variable Chi-Square—Equal Expectations

NPAR TESTS/ CHISQUARE=V85
/EXPECTED=EQUAL or specified categorical frequencies.

Example 4.13—To test whether the observed proportional break-down among the three categories of **V85** (control illegal immigration) is significantly different from an (expected) even distribution among the three. Can we reject the null hypothesis that, in the population from which this sample was drawn, the population is evenly split among the three categories?

NPAR TESTS/CHISQUARE=V85/EXPECTED=EQUAL.

The observed and expected frequencies and their residuals (f_o and f_e) are listed as is the calculated chi-square value.

V85 F1g. U.S. policy goal: control illegal immigration

	Observed N	Expected N	Residual
1	1204	690.0	514.0
3	733	690.0	43.0
5	133	690.0	-557.0
Total	2070		

Test Statistics

	V85 F1g. U.S. policy goal: control illegal immigration
Chi-Square	835.209[a]
df	2
Asymp. Sig.	.000

a. 0 cells (0.0%) have expected frequencies less than 5. The minimum expected cell frequency is 690.0.

For two degrees of freedom (categories-1), a value of 835.209 is large enough to confidently reject the null hypothesis of equality among the three categories.

Form 3: Single Variable Chi-Square—Specified Expectations

You can test your observations against any expected or hypothesized distribution among the three categories. For example, if your research led you to expect a 60%, 20%, 20% division (remember, when calculating chi-square, you must use absolute not relative frequencies-1242, 414, 414):

NPAR TESTS/CHISQUARE=V85/EXPECTED=1242, 414, 414.

Producing the following, also inferentially significant:

V85 F1g. U.S. policy goal: control illegal immigration

	Observed N	Expected N	Residual
1	1204	1242.0	-38.0
3	733	414.0	319.0
5	133	414.0	-281.0
Total	2070		

Test Statistics

	V85 F1g. U.S. policy goal: control illegal immigration
Chi-Square	437.689[a]
df	2
Asymp. Sig.	.000

a. 0 cells (0.0%) have expected frequencies less than 5. The minimum expected cell frequency is 414.0.

Producing this output using the **GUI** interface is much like before, except you will now finish by left-clicking "**Chi-square**." Scroll down the variable list and move it over to the "**Test Variable List**" box. You can then either select "**All categories equal**" as in Example 8.13 or add values until you have your entire expected list as in the following (left-click "**OK**"):

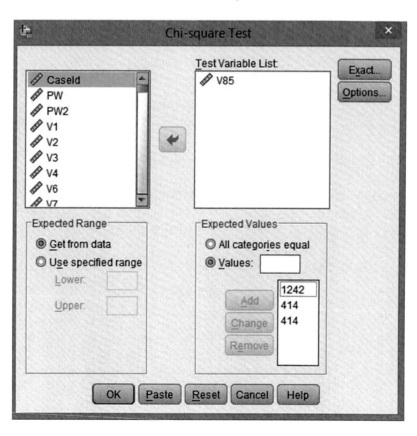

Sample Exercises

ANES2012A

For each exercise, weight the sample by **PW2012**.

1. Using the **BINOMIAL** procedure (Form 1), can you confidently reject the possibility that this sample could have been randomly drawn from a population with a 50/50 proportional breakdown? Run the test for the following attributes for President Obama: **V23, V24, V25, V26**. Answers should be "**NO**," and then three "**YES**." Remember that, although the coding changes, "1" always refers to a positive evaluation.
2. Using the **CHI-SQUARE** procedure (Form 2), can you confidently reject that, in the population from which this sample was (randomly) drawn, the proportional breakdown is not equal among the three categories? Use the following variables: **V34, V35, V40**.

EURO69

For each exercise, weight the sample by **W27**. If analyzing only one country or comparing just two countries against each other, use **W1**.

1. Using the **BINOMIAL** procedure (Form 1), can you confidently reject the possibility that this sample could have been randomly drawn from a population with a 50/50 proportional breakdown? Run the test for the following: **V10**, and, your previously two-category recoded left-right scale (**V25**). Both answers should be "**YES**."
2. Using the **CHI-SQUARE** procedure (Form 2), can you confidently reject that, in the population from which this sample was (randomly) drawn, the proportional breakdown is not equal among the three categories of **EUVOICE**?

CCES2012

For each exercise, weight the sample by **WEIGHT**.

1. Using the **BINOMIAL** procedure (Form 1), can you confidently reject the possibility that this sample could have been randomly drawn from a population with a 50/50 proportional breakdown? Run the test for

the following views about illegal immigration: **V35, V36, V37, V38**. Answers should be "**YES**" for all three. Remember that, in interpreting these findings, "1" is sometimes pro-immigration and sometimes anti-immigration.

2. Repeat step 1 for each of the deficit/tax items: **V43, V44, V45**. You should now have one "**NO**" answer.

3. Using the **CHI-SQUARE** procedure (Form 2), can you confidently reject that, in the population from which this sample was (randomly) drawn, the proportional breakdown is not equal among the three categories? Use the following previously recoded partisan variables: **PID1, PID2, PID3**. Expect an answer of "**YES**" on each.

4.5 CROSSTABS

Function: sets up cross-classification frequencies (also called a contingency table) of two or more variables and provides (if desired) various measures of association and significance.

> **CROSSTABS TABLES=variable or variable list BY variable or variable list.**

For more on this topic, see Chapters 9 and 10 in *Understanding Political Science Statistics: Observations and Expectations in Political Analysis*.

For the sake of consistency, the following directional format (DV first) will be used in all examples:

> **CROSSTABS TABLES=dependent variable(s) BY independent variable(s).**

Example 4.14—to crosstabulate (**ANES2008A**) gender with the party of one's house vote (*always* make sure that all relevant recodes precede the related crosstabulation. None are required here):

> **CROSSTABS TABLES=V68 by V1.**

This will produce the following. The weight variable, **PW2**, was first used. **SPSS** automatically rounds to whole cases after weights are applied. The "Total" figures are often referred to as *marginals*. In this instance, those on the right-most column reflect the total number of those who voted Democratic (category 1) = 690, and Republican (2) = 606. Those on the bottom row, the total number of males (1) = 598 and females (2) = 698. The bottom right corner marginal reflects the total number of respondents represented in the table: 1,296.

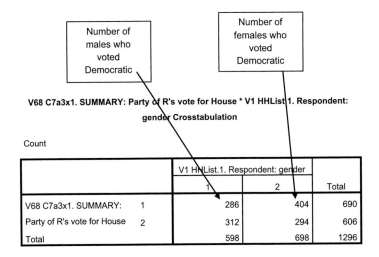

**V68 C7a3x1. SUMMARY: Party of R's vote for House * V1 HHList.1. Respondent:
gender Crosstabulation**

Count

| | | V1 HHList.1. Respondent: gender | | Total |
		1	2	
V68 C7a3x1. SUMMARY:	1	286	404	690
Party of R's vote for House	2	312	294	606
Total		598	698	1296

To use the **GUI** interface, (1) left-click on the "**Analyze**" tab, then
(2) move down to "**Descriptive Statistics**," and (3) slide over and left-click
"**Crosstabs**":

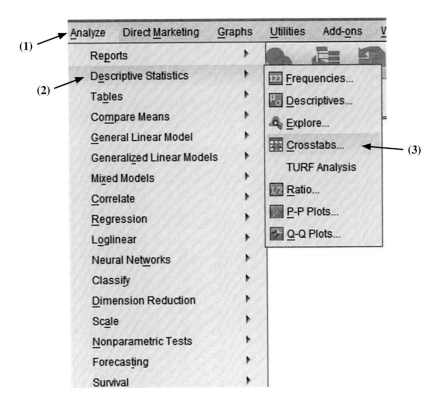

The following dialog box will open:

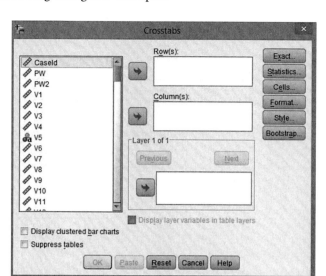

As with the **FREQUENCY** command, use one of the three techniques to move over one variable to the "Rows" space and one to the "Columns." You can enter more variables into each if necessitated by your analysis (see note, p. 53). Which variable(s) you choose to define the **ROWS** and which one(s) to define the **COLUMNS** is a matter of personal choice. The examples in this volume consistently place the independent variable(s) (cause or predictor) as the **COLUMN** variable(s) and the dependent variable(s) (outcome) as the **ROW** variable(s). Our completed Crosstabs dialog box will therefore appear as:

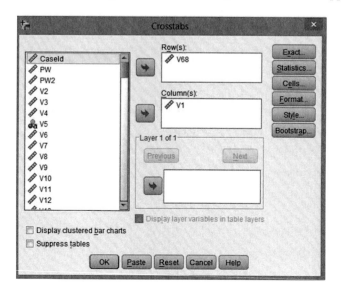

Left-click "**OK**" to produce the chart listed on page 83.

Example 4.15—Because the proportion of females in the sample exceeds the proportion of males (unequal or imbalanced marginals), a comparison between gender must be based not on raw counts or absolute frequencies (example 4.14), but on proportions or percentages. To add standardized percentages, use the **CELL** subcommand to specify which percentage you need (**ROW, COLUMN,** or **TOTAL**). For this example, with the independent variable on the top, defining the columns, we would specify **COL**. That will give us the percentage who voted Democratic both for males and for females.

CROSSTABS TABLES=V68 by V1/CELLS=COUNT COL.

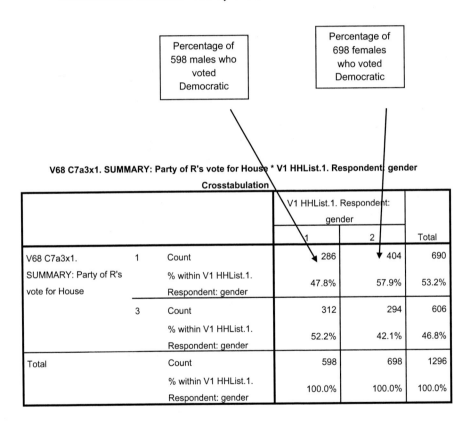

V68 C7a3x1. SUMMARY: Party of R's vote for House * V1 HHList.1. Respondent: gender Crosstabulation

			V1 HHList.1. Respondent: gender		
			1	2	Total
V68 C7a3x1. SUMMARY: Party of R's vote for House	1	Count	286	404	690
		% within V1 HHList.1. Respondent: gender	47.8%	57.9%	53.2%
	3	Count	312	294	606
		% within V1 HHList.1. Respondent: gender	52.2%	42.1%	46.8%
Total		Count	598	698	1296
		% within V1 HHList.1. Respondent: gender	100.0%	100.0%	100.0%

Question: Were females more likely to vote for Democratic House candidates the men?
Answer: Yes. They were 10.1 percentage points more likely to do so (57.9–47.8).

To produce **CELLS** within your **CROSSTABS GUI** menu, before clicking "**OK**," first left-click on the "**Cells**" button.

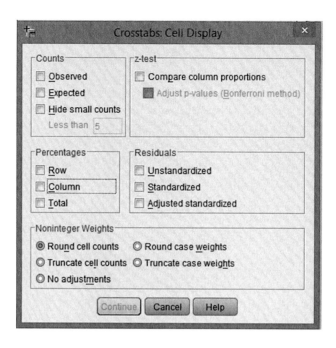

As you can see from this menu, the default is just to produce our original observed or actual frequencies. You can left-click any combination of percentages and unclick the "**Observed**" actual frequencies (although I suggest keeping them so that you can see how the sample breaks down). You can also have the program calculate the "**Expected**" frequencies that are used in the calculation of the chi-square statistic. You can also run a comparison of "**proportions**" test (z-test) that will, below the charts, describe whether the differences between the proportion of men voting Republican (or Democratic) is significantly different ($p \leq .05$) from the proportion of women doing so. After all choices are made, left-click "**Continue**" to return to the original Crosstabs dialogue box. If you have everything you need, left-click "**OK**."

Note: Just as with **FREQUENCIES**, more than one variable can be specified on either side of the **BY**. For example, to check for male-female differences in both House and Senate voting, one can either specify two **CROSSTABS**. . .

CROSSTABS TABLES=V68 by V1/CELLS=COUNT COL.

CROSSTABS TABLES=V69 by V1/CELLS=COUNT COL.

. . . or combine both into one

CROSSTABS TABLES=V68 V69 by V1/CELLS=COUNT COL.

Either will produce two tables, crosstabulating gender by party of house vote and, separately, gender by senate vote.

To compute descriptive and inferential statistics for the table, append the **STATISTICS** subcommand.

The following statistics are supported in the current version of SPSS. You may specify **ALL** or just the ones you want. "**D**" is Somers' D.

CHISQ,PHI,CC,LAMBDA,UC,BTAU,CTAU,RISK,GAMMA,D,KAPPA,ETA,CORR

Example 4.16—For our example, let's just use **CHISQ** (chi-square) and **LAMBDA**.

**CROSSTABS TABLES=V68 by V1/CELLS=COUNT COL
/STATISTICS=LAMBDA CHISQ.**

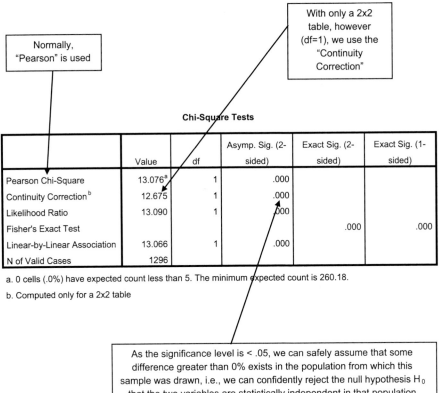

Normally, "Pearson" is used

With only a 2x2 table, however (df=1), we use the "Continuity Correction"

Chi-Square Tests

	Value	df	Asymp. Sig. (2-sided)	Exact Sig. (2-sided)	Exact Sig. (1-sided)
Pearson Chi-Square	13.076[a]	1	.000		
Continuity Correction[b]	12.675	1	.000		
Likelihood Ratio	13.090	1	.000		
Fisher's Exact Test				.000	.000
Linear-by-Linear Association	13.066	1	.000		
N of Valid Cases	1296				

a. 0 cells (.0%) have expected count less than 5. The minimum expected count is 260.18.

b. Computed only for a 2x2 table

As the significance level is < .05, we can safely assume that some difference greater than 0% exists in the population from which this sample was drawn, i.e., we can confidently reject the null hypothesis H_0 that the two variables are statistically independent in that population (males and females give exactly equal support)

Note Carefully: As with statistics already covered, a "significant difference" doesn't necessarily mean that your hypothesis is correct. What if you hypothesized that females were less likely to vote for Democrats than males? As it is not directional, chi-square would still be the same, but in our example the observed data contradict our hypothesis. Reversing the number for males and females would produce the same result.

Lambda produces three measures. The one of greatest importance to us is the non-symmetric (directional) one with V68 (Party of House vote) as the dependent variable. Knowing one's gender helps us reduce our error in guessing the vote proportionately by 4.3%.
Note: Table has been adjusted to fit the page.

Directional Measures

			Value	Asymp. Std. Error[a]	Approx. T[b]	Approx. Sig.
Nominal by Nominal	Lambda	Symmetric	.037	.035	1.030	.303
		V68 C7a3x1. SUMMARY: Party of R's vote for House Dependent	.043	.039	1.064	.287
		V1 HHList.1. Respondent: gender Dependent	.030	.041	.731	.465
	Goodman and Kruskal tau	V68 C7a3x1. SUMMARY: Party of R's vote for House Dependent	.010	.006		.000[c]
		V1 HHList.1. Respondent: gender Dependent	.010	.006		.000[c]

a. Not assuming the null hypothesis.
b. Using the asymptotic standard error assuming the null hypothesis.
c. Based on chi-square approximation.

To produce **STATISTICS** within your **CROSSTABS GUI** menu, before clicking "**OK**," first left-click on the "**Statistics**" button.

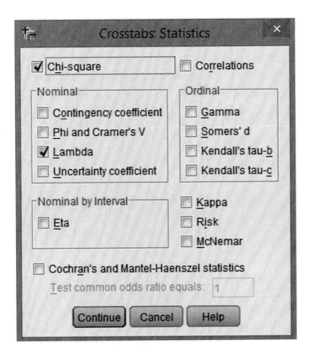

Left-click on the statistics you want produced ("**Chi-square**" and "**lambda**" in our example). After all choices are made, left-click "**Continue**" to return to the original **Crosstabs** dialog box. If you have everything you need, left-click "**OK**."

Example 4.17—To "control" for a third variable in order to test for a spurious relationship, explanatory connection, interaction, or specification effect (produce a separate table for each valid value of that control variable)

> **CROSSTABS TABLES=dependent variable(s)**
> **BY independent variable(s)**
> **BY optional controlling variable(s)**
> **/CELLS=COUNT COL/STATISTICS=CHISQ, LAMBDA.**

Perhaps we want to determine whether gender differences can be explained by one's views about the worth of the Iraq War (**V37**). With two Iraq War view categories, two tables would be produced—House vote by gender for those who felt the Iraq War was worth the cost (category 1 of **V37**) and a separate table for those who thought it wasn't (category 5). If the difference between males and females drops greatly, then one has some reason to believe that differential views about the Iraq War helped cause the gender gap. If the differences stay the same as we original saw (9.9 percentage points), then opinions about the Iraq War do not offer much to explain gender differences in voting. Carry out this procedure to see and interpret the results.

CROSSTABS TABLES=V68 by V1 BY V37/CELLS=COL /STATISTICS=LAMBDA CHISQ.

For the **GUI** version, just move **V37** over into the "**Layer 1 of 1**" box.

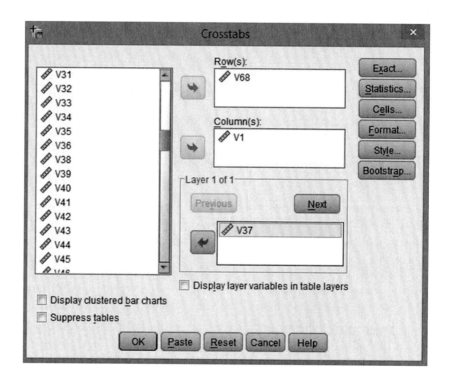

Caution:

Please make sure that if you have a control variable with many categories (age, for example), you first recode it down into two or three categories—otherwise, you wind up with a mother load of tables. The number of separate tables produced *will be equal to the number of categories* of the control variable remaining after recoding. For example, if we wanted to use age (V4) as a control, but did not first recode it, we would have *over 70 separate tables*—one for 17 year olds, one for 18 year olds, etc.

Sample Exercises

ANES2012A

For each exercise, weight the sample by **PW2012**.

1. Were those who felt the election was going to be close (**V31**) more likely to vote (**V64**) than those who felt it would be won by "quite a bit"? Make sure to have the program calculate the relevant percentages (which you will then subtract), chi-square (so that you can test your observations against an expectation or null hypothesis of no difference in the population), lambda, and gamma. Interpret all figures. Note that, given the ordering of the independent and dependent variables, you should anticipate a negative gamma. Remember that, as this is a two-by-two table, the "**continuity correction**" must be used for chi-square.
2. Repeat step 1, but this time make your independent variable **V32** (closeness in state). Compare your results.
3. Using a third, control variable do either results differ much for men versus women?
4. Using a third, control variable (**V32**) how do **V31** and **V32** interact to affect turnout? Don't worry if the results seem a bit counterintuitive.
5. How does one's perception of one's financial status (**V20**) influence how one voted for president (**V66**)? Again, compute percentages, lambda, and gamma, as well as Somers' D. Does it seem that President Obama was rewarded/punished based on this financial evaluation?

Congress2008–2012

1. For any year, use the variable you created with the **IF** (exercise 1) command as your independent variable (e.g. DEM08 or DEM12) and the winning party (e.g., PARTY08 or PARTY12) as your dependent variable. Answer the following question using percentage differences, lambda, Cramer's V, gamma, and Somers' D. Note: If the statement is correct for your year, given the coding of the variables, gamma and Somers' D should be positive.

   Democrats were more likely to win the election if they outspent Republicans. Republicans were equally advantaged.

2. Is there any evidence that leads one to consider the previous relationship to be stronger in those districts with **PCIs** below the mean than above? Repeat the **CROSSTABS** with the recoded **PCI** for your year. If there is, what may be the reason?

EURO69

For each exercise, weight the sample by **W27**. If analyzing only one country or comparing just two countries against each other, use **W1**.

1. Were men or women (**V27**) more likely to feel that being in the EU meant a loss of cultural identity (**V10**)? Make sure to have the program calculate the relevant percentages (which you will then subtract), chi-square (so that you can test your observations against an expectation or null hypothesis of no difference in the population), and lambda. Interpret all figures. Remember that, as this is a two-by-two table, the "**continuity correction**" must be used for chi-square. Again, why is such a small difference statistically significant?

2. Using your two category, recoded **V25** (left-right scale from **RECODE** exercise 3) as your independent variable and your computed **EUPOLICY** (RECODE exercise 3. COMPUTE exercise 1) as your dependent variable, is the following hypothesis confirmed or disconfirmed (at least for this survey)? Calculate and interpret percentage differences and interpret chi-square, lambda, Cramer's V, gamma, and Somers' D. Note that, given the ordering of the independent and dependent variables, you should anticipate a negative gamma and Somers' D.

   Individuals who lean ideologically left are less likely to support common EU policies than those who lean ideologically right.

3. Using a third, control variable (**V27**) do either results differ much for men versus women?

4. Special combination:

   STEP 1: Select any two countries using the **SELECT IF** command. For example, to select only Spain and Portugal:

   SELECT IF (COUNTRY EQ 6 or 14).

   STEP 2: As you will be comparing two countries, use the **W1** weight.
   STEP 3: Using a **CROSSTABS** procedure, do the citizens of your two countries differ on their support of common EU policies (**EUPOLICY**)?

CCES2012

For each exercise, weight the sample by **WEIGHT**.

1. Are those respondents who themselves or who had family members who served in the military (**V17**) more or less likely to agree (not a mistake) with U.S. intervention in Iraq (**V26**) and Afghanistan (**V27**)? Make sure

to have the program calculate the relevant percentages (which you will then subtract), chi-square (so that you can test your observations against an expectation or null hypothesis of no difference in the population), lambda, and gamma. Interpret all figures. Note that, given the ordering of the independent and dependent variables, you should anticipate a negative gamma if they were more likely and a positive gamma if they were less likely.

2. Using a third, control variable do either results differ much for men versus women?

3. Using your previous two-category "health insurance" variable, were those with health insurance more likely to have excellent health and less likely to be in poor health? Can you think of another variable that might reduce the degree to which that relationship is confirmed (Hint: think about how some individuals automatically receive health insurance.)

CROSSNAT

1. Using a simple **CROSSTABS** procedure, answer the following question:

   *Are countries that limit party spending (**IDEA_LPS**) more likely to provide direct funding to them (**IDEA_DPFP**) than countries that do not limit spending?*

   Use percentage differences, lambda, gamma, and Somers' D to help answer the question. The directional measures should be positive if the question is answered affirmatively.

2. Is there a difference in this relationship between countries with a unicameral and a bicameral legislature?

4.6 REGRESSION (SIMPLE LINEAR)

Function: Tests for the linear relationship (direction and value) between a dependent (outcome) variable and one or more independent (potentially causal) variables. The regression equation is based upon minimizing the sum of the squared differences between the observed values on the dependent variable and the values predicted by the calculated regression equation. The form and examples will only demonstrate the simplest form of this statistical procedure.

For more on this topic, see Chapters 11 and 12 in *Understanding Political Science Statistics: Observations and Expectations in Political Analysis.*

This is the simplest representation of the procedure's command. The following statistics will be calculated as a default and should give you all the information needed: **R, ANOVA, COEFF**. The **METHOD** subcommand has different options: **ENTER, STEPWISE, REMOVE, FORWARD, BACKWARDS.**

REGRESSION/VARIABLES = all variables in the model
/DEPENDENT = dependent variable in the model
/METHOD=ENTER.

Example 4.18—To test whether there is a linear association between the proportion of individuals 65 and older (**PER65**) in a district and the district's vote for Barack Obama (**OBAMA**) in 2008 (**CONGRESS2008**).

REGRESSION /VARIABLES = PER65 OBAMA
/DEPENDENT = OBAMA/METHOD=ENTER.

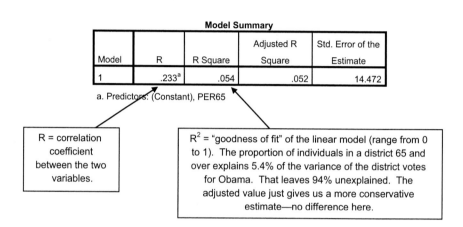

Model Summary

Model	R	R Square	Adjusted R Square	Std. Error of the Estimate
1	.233[a]	.054	.052	14.472

a. Predictors: (Constant), PER65

R = correlation coefficient between the two variables.

R^2 = "goodness of fit" of the linear model (range from 0 to 1). The proportion of individuals in a district 65 and over explains 5.4% of the variance of the district votes for Obama. That leaves 94% unexplained. The adjusted value just gives us a more conservative estimate—no difference here.

ANOVA[b]

Model		Sum of Squares	df	Mean Square	F	Sig.
1	Regression	5204.085	1	5204.085	24.849	.000[a]
	Residual	90683.102	433	209.430		
	Total	95887.186	434			

a. Predictors: (Constant), PER65

b. Dependent Variable: Obama

Note: Notice that the Total sum of squares (original variation on **OBAMA**) minus the Regression Sum of Squares (explained by **PER65**) equals the Residual Sum of Squares. Also notice that if you perform the following calculation (Total – Residual)/Total you will come up with the R^2 value. Meaning? Like Lambda, regression performs a proportional reduction of (squared) errors measurement. Knowing the variance on **PER65** reduces your error in guessing the variance on **OBAMA** by 5.4%.

Now for the good part. The following table defines the intercept and slope of the linear regression equation. Note that we can use the phrase "For every 1% increase" because PER65 is measured as a percent. If this was instead mean age, then it would be for every 1 year increase ...":

$$\text{OBAMA} = 68.911\% - 1.210 \times \text{PER65}$$

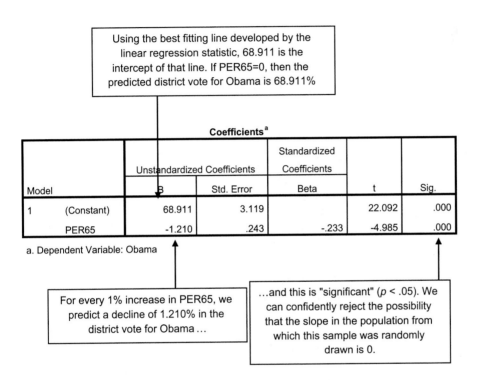

Using the best fitting line developed by the linear regression statistic, 68.911 is the intercept of that line. If PER65=0, then the predicted district vote for Obama is 68.911%

Coefficients[a]

Model		Unstandardized Coefficients B	Std. Error	Standardized Coefficients Beta	t	Sig.
1	(Constant)	68.911	3.119		22.092	.000
	PER65	-1.210	.243	-.233	-4.985	.000

a. Dependent Variable: Obama

For every 1% increase in PER65, we predict a decline of 1.210% in the district vote for Obama ...

...and this is "significant" ($p < .05$). We can confidently reject the possibility that the slope in the population from which this sample was randomly drawn is 0.

Note: This author, a member of the old school, believes that significance is only a fully useful concept if this was a random sample of a larger population (which it is not). If it were, we could state that, although **PER65** doesn't seem to explain much, the coefficient is still large enough for us to confidently *reject* the possibility that the proportion of district voters 65 and older explains none of the variation of the vote for Obama in the population from which this sample was randomly drawn. There is a school of statistical theory that accepts significance levels as a surrogate way of measuring the importance of a relationship, or one that starts with the premise that all data are random (see text, Chapter 7). Obviously, all schools will agree that significance levels are meaningful with random, equiprobable surveys.

Question: Using the regression formula, what would you predict Obama's vote to be if the proportion of those 65 and older was 20%?

Answer: 68.911% − 1.210 × 20% = 44.911%

Example 4.19—What if we add the percentage of district individuals classified racially as **BLACK** to the equation. Do we improve our predictive power? Which variable (**PER65** or **BLACK**) explains more of the variance of the vote for Obama?

REGRESSION/VARIABLES = PER65 BLACK OBAMA /DEPENDENT = OBAMA/METHOD=ENTER.

Let's look at only two parts of the resulting output.

Model Summary

Model	R	R Square	Adjusted R Square	Std. Error of the Estimate
1	.491[a]	.241	.238	12.976

a. Predictors: (Constant), BLACK, PER65

Adding the variable BLACK increases our explanation of the variance from 5.4% to 24.1%.

ANOVA[b]

Model		Sum of Squares	df	Mean Square	F	Sig.
1	Regression	23143.144	2	11571.572	68.719	.000[a]
	Residual	72744.043	432	168.389		
	Total	95887.186	434			

a. Predictors: (Constant), BLACK, PER65

b. Dependent Variable: Obama

The intercept now changes to 57.315% (PER65=0, BLACK=0)

Each slope is significantly different from 0.

Coefficients[a]

Model		Unstandardized Coefficients B	Std. Error	Standardized Coefficients Beta	t	Sig.
1	(Constant)	57.315	3.014		19.015	.000
	PER65	-.727	.223	-.140	-3.263	.001
	BLACK	.443	.043	.442	10.322	.000

a. Dependent Variable: Obama

For every 1% increase in PER65, we predict a .727% drop in the district vote for Obama. For every 1% increase in BLACK, we predict a .443% increase in the vote for Obama

Beta, the standardized coefficient, is larger (absolute value) for BLACK than it is for PER65. The proportion of Black individuals in a district is more important than the proportion 65 and older in statistically explaining how well Obama did.

Question: What is the predicted district vote for Obama if **PER65** = 20% and **BLACK** = 35%?
    Answer: 58.28%

Example 4.20—You can produce different regression outputs for different subsets of cases. For example, if you wished to see if the effects of **PER65** on Obama were different for districts won by Democrats and districts won by Republicans, you would click on "**Party08**" and place it into the "**Selection Variable**" space. You will then be asked to specify a "**Rule**." First enter the number "1," which refers to Democratic-won districts only. Left-click "**OK**." After the regression equations are produced, go back to that Rule, and specify "2" so that only the Republican districts are included. If you have carried this out properly, you will have two sets of results:

> **REGRESSION /VARIABLES = PER65 OBAMA**
> **/DEPENDENT = OBAMA/METHOD=ENTER**
> **/SELECT = PARTY08 EQ 1.**

> **REGRESSION /VARIABLES = PER65 OBAMA**
> **/DEPENDENT = OBAMA/METHOD=ENTER**
> **/SELECT = PARTY08 EQ 2.**

Districts won by Democrats:

Model Summary

Model	R Party08 = 1 (Selected)	R Square	Adjusted R Square	Std. Error of the Estimate
1	.398[a]	.158	.155	12.392

a. Predictors: (Constant), PER65

ANOVA[a,b]

Model		Sum of Squares	df	Mean Square	F	Sig.
1	Regression	7361.924	1	7361.924	47.939	.000[c]
	Residual	39160.279	255	153.570		
	Total	46522.202	256			

a. Dependent Variable: Obama

b. Selecting only cases for which Party08 = 1

c. Predictors: (Constant), PER65

Coefficients[a,b]

Model		Unstandardized Coefficients		Standardized Coefficients		
		B	Std. Error	Beta	t	Sig.
1	(Constant)	86.428	3.684		23.458	.000
	PER65	-2.013	.291	-.398	-6.924	.000

a. Dependent Variable: Obama

b. Selecting only cases for which Party08 =   1

Districts won by Republicans:

Model Summary

Model	R Party08 = 2 (Selected)	R Square	Adjusted R Square	Std. Error of the Estimate
1	.004[a]	.000	-.006	8.185

a. Predictors: (Constant), PER65

ANOVA[a,b]

Model		Sum of Squares	df	Mean Square	F	Sig.
1	Regression	.182	1	.182	.003	.959[c]
	Residual	11791.054	176	66.995		
	Total	11791.236	177			

a. Dependent Variable: Obama

b. Selecting only cases for which Party08 =   2

c. Predictors: (Constant), PER65

Coefficients[a,b]

Model		Unstandardized Coefficients		Standardized Coefficients		
		B	Std. Error	Beta	t	Sig.
1	(Constant)	42.454	2.581		16.446	.000
	PER65	.010	.197	.004	.052	.959

a. Dependent Variable: Obama

b. Selecting only cases for which Party08 =   2

Question: Does **PER65** better explain the variance of Obama in Democratic or Republican districts? Why or why not?

Note: With an older version of **SPSS**, the **/SELECT** subcommand does not exist. To produce the same output, you would have to enter the following:

> **TEMPORARY.**
> **SELECT IF (PARTY08 EQ 1).**
> **REGRESSION/VARIABLES = PER65 OBAMA**
>   **/DEPENDENT = OBAMA/METHOD=ENTER.**
> **TEMPORARY.**
> **SELECT IF (PARTY08 EQ 2).**
> **REGRESSION /VARIABLES = PER65 OBAMA**
>   **/DEPENDENT = OBAMA/METHOD=ENTER.**

Note: A separate procedure, **CORRELATIONS**, will produce the Pearson product moment coefficient, r, for two or a set of variables. For any two variable comparison, r will be equal to the square root of R^2. However, direction will be taken into account (+/-). The slope of your regression will indicate that direction.

The regression **GUI** is rather straightforward. Let's start with our simplest example, Example 4.18—

> **REGRESSION /VARIABLES = PER65 OBAMA**
>   **/DEPENDENT = OBAMA/METHOD=ENTER.**

To produce this output using the **GUI** interface, (1) left-click on "**Analyze**," (2) slide down to "**Regression**," and then (3) slide over to and left-click "**Linear**":

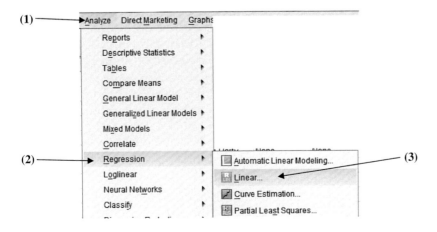

The following dialog box will appear:

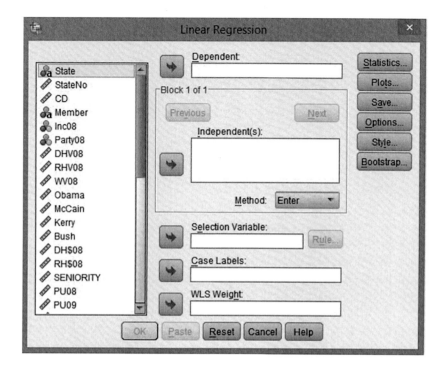

Using any of the methods previously listed, move "**Obama**" into the "**Dependent**" frame, and "**PER65**" into the "**Independent(s)**" frame. **ENTER** is the default variable input method. Left-click "**OK**" and the first regression output will be produced. If you have more than one independent variable, they can both be placed in the **Independent(s)** frame.

In example 4.20, you wished to see if the effects of **PER65** on Obama were different for districts won by Democrats and districts won by Republicans (**PARTY08**). You would click on "**Party08**" and place it into the "**Selection Variable**" space. You will then be asked to specify a "**Rule**." First enter the number "1," which refers to Democratic-won districts only. Left-click "**OK**." After the regression equations are produced, go back to that **Rule**, and specify "2" so that only the Republican districts are included.

Plots

This linear regression procedure, either in Syntax or **GUI** mode, can produce many more statistics, certain plots, and differing methods of entering the independent variables chosen (if choosing more than one). Refer to your text or instructor on when to use each of these possibilities. The "**Plots**" button does not, unfortunately, produce the standard, two-variable scatter plot with the regression line included.

To do so, one must (1) left-click on "**Graphs**" and (2) slide the cursor down to "**Regression Variable Plots**":

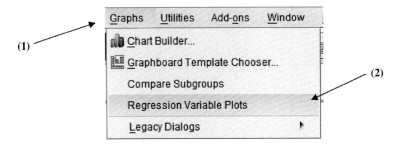

The following will appear:

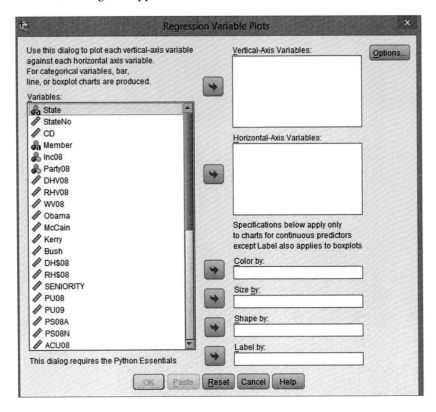

By convention, the y-axis (vertical) is used for the dependent variable (**Obama**) and the x-axis (horizontal) for the independent variable (**PER65**). Type those two into their relevant spaces.

Several ways exist to place the best-fitting regression line into the plot area. The easiest is to left-click on the "**Options**" button. Within that dialogue box, left-click on the "**Linear**" box in the "**Scatterplot Fit Lines**" section. Left-click "**Continue.**" The original **Regression** dialog box will reappear. Left-click on "**OK.**" You should see the following:

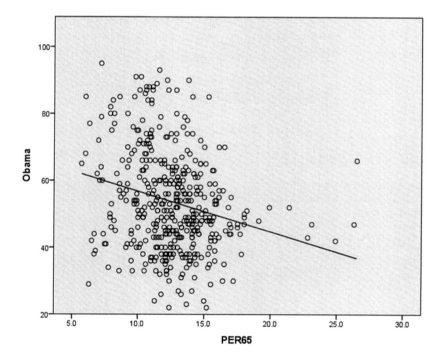

Notice that the equation for the regression line does not appear. If you want that to be placed within your chart you can copy the chart into a Word or other text processing document (see the next section) and add it by way of inserting a text box. Alternately, you can double left-click anywhere within your chart area. This will produce a "**chart editor**" dialog box:

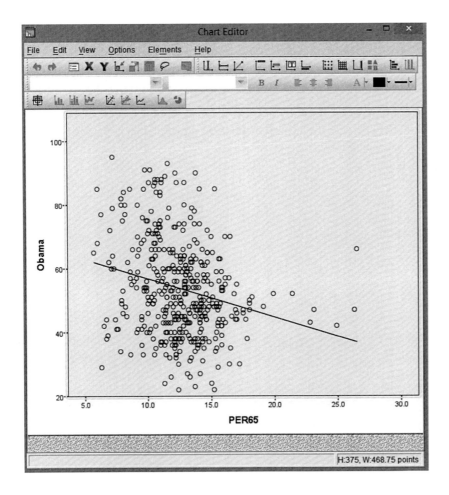

By left-clicking on the "**Options**" tab, you will be given the opportunity to insert a text box and then replace the word "**Textbox**" with your regression equation:

$$\textbf{OBAMA=68.911\%-1.210 x PER65}$$

You can alter the way the graph looks in many ways. For example, if you placed **Party08** (the winning party in the election) in the "**Color by**" slot, you would have one color for districts won by Democrats, one for districts won by Republicans. Repeating the steps we used in creating the original chart with the best-fitting regression line inserted, and left-clicking the button marked "**Fit line for each categorical color group**," produces the best-fitting regression lines for Democratic districts and, separately, districts won by Republicans:

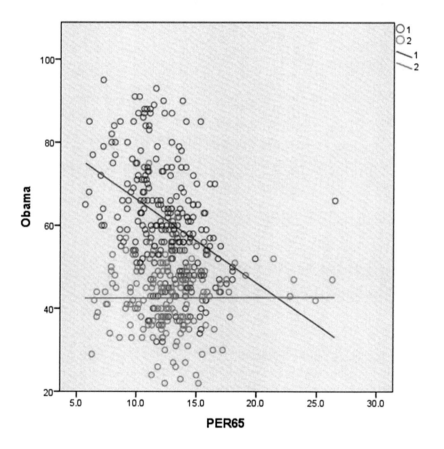

Without color, of course, you would not be able to easily differentiate the type of districts, but you could, as before, create a separate scatter-plot for each set of districts.

In earlier versions of **SPSS**, the "**Regression Variables Plots**" procedure does not exist. Instead one must resort to a different method. To do so, one must (1) left-click on "**Graphs**," (2) slide the cursor down to "**Legacy Dialogs**," and then (3) move over and left-click "**Scatter/Dot**":

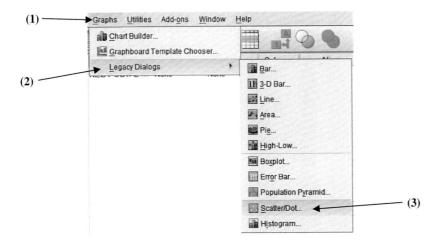

You will see the following:

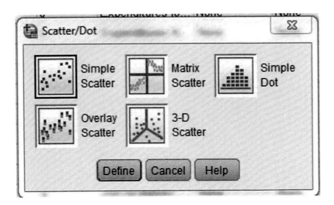

The "Simple **Scatter**" plot should be outlined. If not, left-click on the box. Left-click on the "**Define**" button:

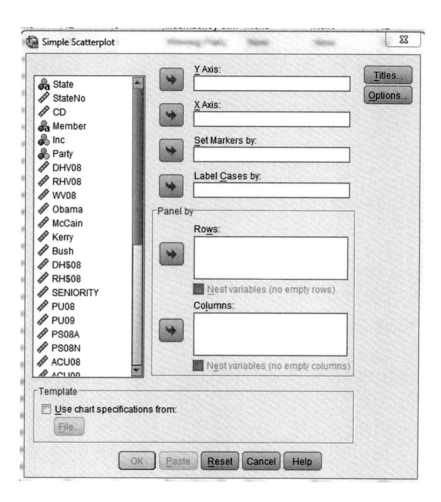

Move "**Obama**" into the "**Y Axis**" field and "**PER65**" into the "**X Axis**" field. Left-click "**OK**." Double left-click on the chart in your output. This is the easiest method to produce a chart editor alongside your output chart:

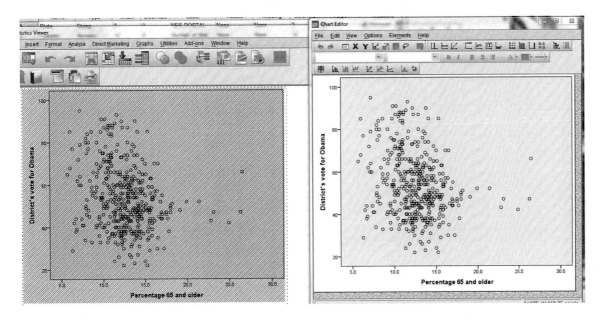

On the Chart Editor, left click on the fifth graphic on the bottom of the toolbar. This will insert your regression line and list the R^2 value.

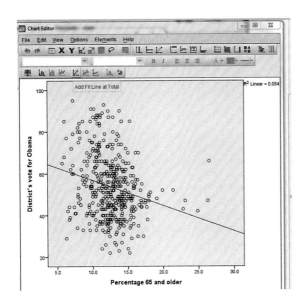

If you wish to insert the regression equation into the plot, you can left-click on the "**Options**" tab, and choose (left-click) "**Text Box**." Replace the term "**Textbox**" in the frame with your equation:

$$\text{OBAMA} = 68.911\% - 1.210 \times \text{PER65}.$$

Resize and move your equation to an appropriate location by the regression line:

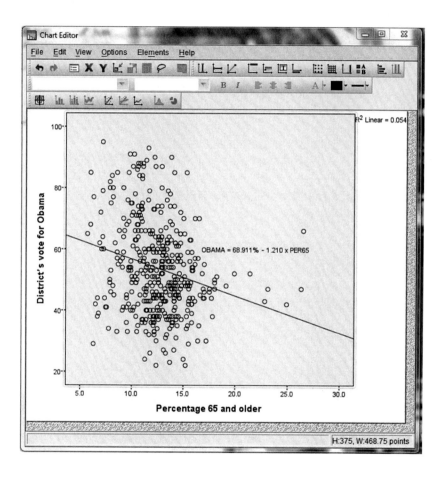

Close the Chart Editor and the line and equation will appear in your output.

Sample Exercises

ANES2012A

For each exercise, weight the sample by **PW2012**.

1. Using a simple, two-variable linear regression, do your results confirm or disconfirm the following hypothesis for 2012? Your answer should be "No," but interpret the unstandardized slope and R^2 values. Also, is the slope significantly different from 0?

   *The cooler one feels toward Big Business (**V75B**), the warmer one feels toward the Tea Party (**V81T**), and the relationship is negative and linear.*

2. Follow up on step 1, add in feelings toward Blacks (**V78**). Interpret the individual unstandardized slopes and their t values, compare the standardized ones, and interpret the R^2 value. Does adding **V78** change the values much? Which of your two independent variables is more important in explaining variation on the Tea Party thermometer?

3. Follow up on step 1, and using the **/SELECT =** subcommand, is the relationship different between those who are angry at President Obama (**V23**) or not? Now, enter V23 as a separate independent, dummy variable. Interpret those results. Does **V23** or feelings toward big business better explain feelings toward the Tea Party?

Congress2008–2012

1. Using a simple, two-variable linear regression, do your results confirm or disconfirm the following hypothesis for any year? Interpret the unstandardized slope and R^2 values. Remember that the unstandardized slope will seem extremely low, but that is only because the variation in $ is much greater than marginal victory percentages. **SPENDDIFF** and **WINDDIFF** were created in **COMPUTE** exercise 1 and 2.

   *The more that Democrats spend in comparison to Republicans (**SPENDDIFF**) the greater will be their winning margin over Republicans (**WINDIFF**), and the relationship is positive and linear.*

2. Using a simple two-variable regression, answer the following question comparing results from 2008 and 2012.

As the percentage of Hispanics in a district increases, so should the Democratic vote, and the relationship is positive and linear.

You will first need to **COMPUTE** two new variables. **DEMDIFF** was already treated in **COMPUTE** exercise 4 (**DHV12-DHV08**). You will also need to compute your independent variable, call it **HISDIFF**, which equals **HISPANIC12-HISPANIC08**.

3. Follow up on step 1, and using the **/SELECT** = subcommand, is the relationship different in those districts with **PCIs** below the mean than above? Now, enter that recoded **PCI** as a separate independent, dummy variable. Interpret those results. Does **PCI** or spending differences explain more of the variance of **WINDIFF?** Discuss all relevant measures.

EURO69

For each exercise, weight the sample by **W27**. If analyzing only one country or comparing just two countries against each other, use **W1**.

1. Using a simple, two-variable linear regression, do your results confirm or disconfirm the following hypothesis? Interpret the unstandardized slope and R^2 values. Also, is the slope significantly different from 0?

The older one is, the less likely one is to believe in the seriousness of global warming.

2. Follow up on step 1, and using the **/SELECT** = subcommand, is the relationship different between left- and right-leaning individuals (recoded **V25**) or not? Now, enter **V25** as a separate independent, dummy variable. Interpret those results. Does ideology or age better explain perceptions about global warming? Discuss all measures.

CCES2012

For each exercise, weight the sample by **WEIGHT**.

1. Using a simple, two-variable linear regression, do your results confirm or disconfirm the following hypothesis for 2012? Your answer should be a cautioned "**YES**," but interpret the unstandardized slope and R^2 values. Also, is the slope significantly different from 0?

*The older one is (**V5**) the more likely one is to prefer solving state budget deficits with cuts than taxes (**V60**) and the relationship is positive and linear.*

2. Follow up on #1, and using the **/SELECT** = subcommand, is the relationship different between men and women (**V1**). Why or why not? Now, enter **V1** as a separate independent, dummy variable. Interpret those results. Does gender or age better explain one's allocation choice for solving budget deficits?

3. Follow up to **COMPUTE 1** and 2: Is there a linear relationship between income and candidate proximity (use **PROXIMITY,** not **PROXIMITY2**)? Using **REGRESSION**, fully explain your answer.

Note: Some might balk at using **V14** (Family Income) in a regression analysis as the 15 categories are not truly interval. The midpoints are not equally spaced, nor are the proportions in each category roughly equal.

CROSSNAT

1. Using a simple two-variable linear regression, is the following hypothesis confirmed or disconfirmed?

   There is a positive, linear relationship between health expenditures per capita and life expectancy.

   Interpret the unstandardized slope and R^2 values.

2. Special combination:

   Step 1: Using a **COMPUTE** function, calculate the difference between male and female literacy rates (**WDI_LITM- WDI_LITF**). Call the new variable **LITDIFF**. The higher the value, the greater the literacy of men compared to women.

   Step 2: Is there a negative, linear relationship between **LITTDIFF** and the percentage of seats held by women in the lower house (**IDEA_SWLH**)?

3. Conduct a multivariate regression procedure, with voter turnout for parliament as the dependent variable (**IDEA_VTVAP_PA**), total literacy rate as one dependent variable, and compulsory voting (**CVOTE_L**) as the second, dummy variable. Which independent variable is more important in explaining voting turnout? Interpret the different slopes and R^2 value.

4. Following up on step 3, is the relationship between literacy and turnout subdued when voting is compulsory?

Executing Your Syntax and Saving Your Output

As with everything **SPSS**, there are a number of ways to execute (run) your syntax commands to get your output. Only one method will be shown.

Open your **SPSS** program. If this is your first time doing so, you will see a blank spreadsheet. Left-click on the "**File**" button and then move the cursor over to "**New**" and then "**Syntax**."

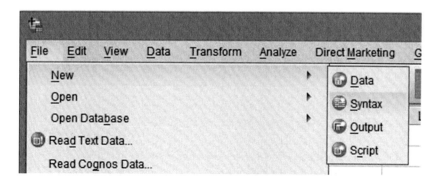

You should see the following:

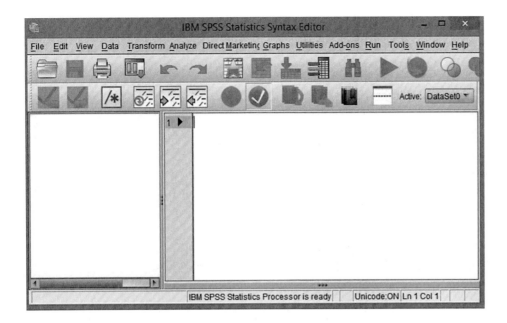

The following was used to access the data file on my computer, located on my desktop. It might be different for you. Placing an * at the beginning of a line just treats that line as a comment. It doesn't process any data but it may help you to keep track of what you are doing. Previous versions of SPSS treated an * as a TEMPORARY transformation. Be careful if you have an older version of SPSS. If you do, replace the * with the word COMMENT into the open space on the right of the editor:

*A Trial Run.
GET FILE='C:\Users\MyBuild\Desktop\ANES2008A.sav'.
WEIGHT BY PW2.
FREQUENCIES VARIABLES=V1.

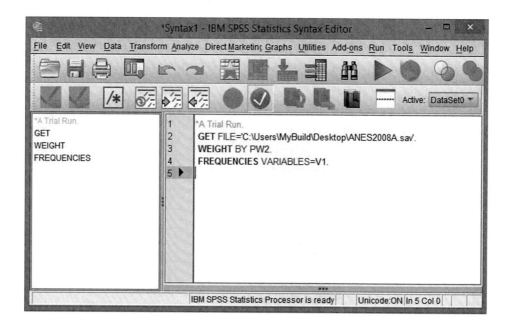

To run all of your syntax, you can either highlight it all, and then left-click on the green ("**Run Selection**") arrow (next to the binoculars). As an alternative, do not highlight your syntax. Instead, move the cursor (do not hold down a mouse button as you do this) over to the **RUN** button above the green arrow.

(1) Right click the **RUN** button by holding down the left mouse button as you are over it. (2) Click on "**All**."

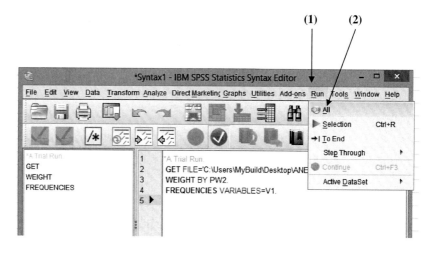

If there was a problem with your syntax, a box will appear specifying the type of problem. Write that information down. If you can figure out the error, fix it in your syntax. I suggest you start your "run" from the beginning (**GET**), thus giving you a clean slate. Students run into the most problems when they incorrectly **RECODE** a variable and then **RECODE** it again. Starting from the **GET** command (or retrieving the original file again as described on pp. 12–13) eliminates this problem. **SPSS** always creates a temporary file for you to use, saving the original.

If everything ran smoothly, you will have a table as shown below. It will be listed in a separate output (.spv) window. Try out this simple test to make sure you can operate **SPSS** successfully.

Statistics

V1 HHList.1. Respondent: gender

N	Valid	2102
	Missing	0

V1 HHList.1. Respondent: gender

		Frequency	Percent	Valid Percent	Cumulative Percent
Valid	1	1008	48.0	48.0	48.0
	2	1093	52.0	52.0	100.0
	Total	2102	100.0	100.0	

Once you have successfully run all of your instructions (syntax) and are satisfied with your output, you can save the output results in a number of ways.

Option 1: capture an image

Use the snipping (scissors) program that comes with Windows 7 or 8 or the GET-CAPTURE procedure with MAC OS, clip the output that you would like to use (I suggest table by table), and then paste it into a Word document. With Mac Snow Leopard, you first have to copy what you captured before it can be pasted (I'm sure the Mac-savvy among you know how best to do this). The problem with this method is that you cannot type labels or such within your output as you will be able to with the next two sets of options.

Option 2: Export each section of your output directly to a Word document

With the output window opened, right-click on the corner of any of your tables or other information:

V1 HHList.1. Respondent: gender				
		Frequency	Percent	Valid Percent
Valid	1	1008	48.0	48.0
	2	1093	52.0	52.0
	Total	2102	100.0	100.0

Cut
Copy
Copy Special...
Paste After
Create/Edit Autoscript...
Style Output...
Export...

You can then paste that section right into your Word document. You can highlight, underline, change fonts, delete information, reformat, or add labels to that pasted section. The same applies to Option 3.

Option 3: Export the entire output document into Word
Click on "File" then "Export."

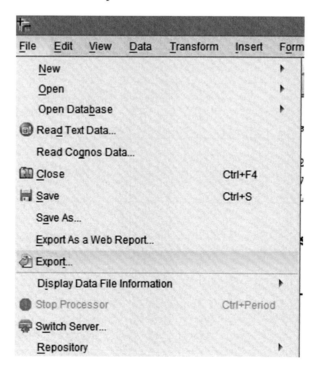

For Option 3 a window will open allowing you to save the file in a number of formats (choose "Word/RTF"), give it a name, and find it a location. You can either type the information directly into the open space, or browse for a location and then type the name (.doc will automatically be added if you chose to export it as a Word document).

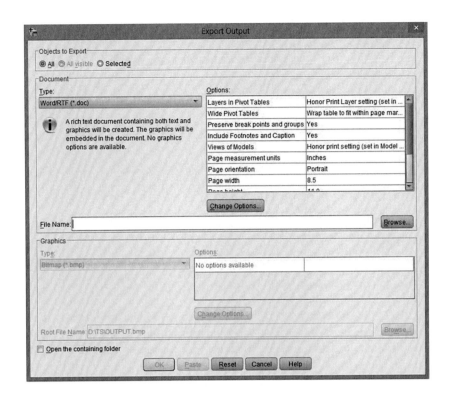

A number of options exist for formatting your output. Play around with some of them to see what best suits your needs.

The instructions for MAC OS will be the same, except with some difference in the graphics.

As a last step, I suggest that you save your syntax file (.sps). Left-click "**File**," then "**Save**" or "**Save As**." A window will open that will allow you to save that file wherever you want (I suggest a USB or cloud drive so that your instructor can review it if you have errors). Give it a name that matches your exercise (e.g., genderfreq1). The suffix .spv will automatically be added. You can then reopen this file another time in SPSS. Close out all of your files. Play it safe: when the program asks if you want to "Save changes to the following dataset?" click "**No**." This will guarantee that you retain the original file even if you never protected it (pp. 4–6).

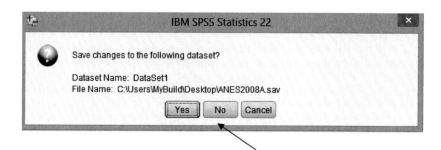

Appendix A

Codebooks for Data Files (SPSS.sav Files)

ANES2008A: a subset of the 2008 National Election Study—all respondents

ANES2008S: a subset of **ANES2008A** suitable for use with the student version of **SPSS** and **SMALL STATA**

ANES2012A: a subset of the 2012 National Election Study—all respondents

ANES2012S: a subset of **ANES2012A** suitable for use with the student version of **SPSS** and **STAT SE**

CONGRESS2008: a selection of political and demographic data for all 435 Congressional districts

CONGRESS2008–2012: a comprehensive file tracking changes during the 2010 midterm and post redistricting U.S. House (2014 results will be added when available)

EURO69: a subset of the March–May 2008 (**EB69:2**) data set—all respondents from then current EU member nations

EURO69D, EURO69H, EURO69I: single nation (Denmark, Hungary, Italy) data file suitable for use with the student version of **SPSS** and **SMALL STATA**

CCES2012: a subset of the 2012 Cooperative Congressional Election Study—all respondents

CCES2012I, CCES2012M: single state (Indiana, Maryland) data files suitable for use with the student version of **SPSS** and **SMALL STATA**

CROSSNAT: a multi-national file containing country-specific political, economic, and demographic variables

NOTE: Value labels, with the exception of state or country names, have been eliminated from these files. Although the author of this manual understands the clarity provided by labels, he also has experienced three decades of student confusion after recoding a variable while maintaining the old, non-recoded labels. Students can enter labels into their output once converted to a word processing program.

For example, look at **V10** in the **ANES 2008** codebook. If a student recodes that variable into three categories (approve, neither, disapprove), the labels will still read:

1. Approve strongly
2. Approve not strongly
3. Neither/DK

A1: ANES2008 CODEBOOK

NOTE: Two data files are associated with this codebook.

ANES2008A.SAV includes all of the following variables and all of the survey respondents (N = 2012).

ANES2008S.SAV includes only the variables whose names are in *italics*, and only those respondents who claim to have voted for both President and the House of Representatives (N = 1180).

This data set can be analyzed with the reduced, student version of **SPSS** and **SMALL STATA**.

Note that, with ANES2008.sav, you will not be able to answer any questions about why someone voted (or not) as nonvoters have been eliminated.

Variable Name	Variable Label
	Value. Value Label
PW	SAMPLE WEIGHT—POST-ELECTION
	0. No Post-election interview
PW2	WEIGHT ADJUSTED FOR UNINTENTIONAL OVERSAMPLING OF WOMEN

PRE-ELECTION INTERVIEW PHASE:

V1   GENDER
              1.   Male
              2.   Female

V2   RACE
              1.   White
              2.   Black/African-American
              3.   Other

V3   LATINO
              1.   Latino
              2.   Not Latino

V4   AGE (actual coded)   Mean = 46.5   Median = 46.0
              17.   17 years old (18 by Oct 30, 2008)
              18.   18 years old
              . . .
              . . .
              90.   90 years old or older

V5   State Postal Code (e.g., AK = Alaska)

V6   CENSUS REGION
              1.   Northeast
              2.   North Central
              3.   South
              4.   West

V7   How much has R (survey respondent) thought about
              election for President?
              1.   Quite a lot
              2.   Only a little

V8   Did R vote for President in 2004?
              1.   Yes, voted
              2.   No, didn't vote

V9   Recall of last (2004) Presidential vote choice
              1.   John Kerry
              2.   George W. Bush

V10   Approve/disapprove Pres handling job
              1.   Approve strongly
              2.   Approve not strongly

3. Neither/DK
4. Disapprove not strongly
5. Disapprove strongly

V11   Approve/disapprove Pres handling economy
1. Approve strongly
2. Approve not strongly
3. Neither/DK
4. Disapprove not strongly
5. Disapprove strongly

V12   Approve/disapprove Pres handling foreign relations
1. Approve strongly
2. Approve not strongly
3. Neither/DK
4. Disapprove not strongly
5. Disapprove strongly

V13   Approve/disapprove Pres handling health care
1. Approve strongly
2. Approve not strongly
3. Neither/DK
4. Disapprove not strongly
5. Disapprove strongly

V14   Approve/disapprove Pres handling war in Iraq
1. Approve strongly
2. Approve not strongly
3. Neither/DK
4. Disapprove not strongly
5. Disapprove strongly

I'd like to get your feelings toward some of our political leaders and other people who are in the news these days. I'll read the name of a person and I'd like you to rate that person using something we call the feeling thermometer. Ratings between 50 degrees and 100 degrees mean that you feel favorable and warm toward the person. Ratings between 0 degrees and 50 degrees mean that you don't feel favorable toward the person and that you don't care too much for that person. You would rate the person at the 50 degree mark if you don't feel particularly warm or cold toward the person. If we come to a person whose name you don't recognize, you don't need to rate that person. Just tell me and we'll move on to the next one.

V15   Feeling Thermometer: President (GWB)
          Mean = 40.6 Median = 40.0*

V16   Feeling Thermometer: Democratic Presidential
               candidate   Mean= 57.7 Median = 60.0

V17   Feeling Thermometer: Republican Presidential
               candidate   Mean = 51.9 Median = 50.0

V18   Feeling Thermometer: Democratic Party
                   Mean = 56.9 Median = 60.0

V19   Feeling Thermometer: Republican Party
                   Mean = 48.1 Median = 50.0

V20   R better/worse off than 1 year ago
               1.   Better
               2.   The Same
               3.   Worse

V21   Will R be financially better/worse off one year from now?
               1.   Better
               2.   The Same
               3.   Worse

V22   Does R have health insurance?
               1.   Yes
               2.   No

V23   Affect for Democratic Pres candidate: angry
               0.   Yes
               1.   No

V24   Affect for Democratic Pres candidate: hopeful
               0.   No
               1.   Yes

V25   Affect for Democratic Pres candidate: afraid
               0.   Yes
               1.   No

V26   Affect for Democratic Pres candidate: proud
               0.   No
               1.   Yes

V27   Affect for Republican Pres candidate: angry
               0.   Yes
               1.   No

V28 Affect for Republican Pres candidate: hopeful
    0. No
    1. Yes

V29 Affect for Republican Pres candidate: afraid
    0. Yes
    1. No

V30 Affect for Republican Pres candidate: proud
    0. No
    1. Yes

V31 Will Pres race be a close or will (winner) win by a lot
    1. Will be close
    2. Win by quite a bit

V32 Will Pres race be close in state
    1. Will be close
    2. Win by quite a bit

V33 Economy better worse in last year
    1. Much better
    2. Somewhat better
    3. Stayed about the same
    4. Somewhat worse
    5. Much worse

V34 Which party better: handling nation's economy
    1. Democrats
    2. Either/Neither/DK
    3. Republicans

V35 During last year, U.S. position in world weaker/stronger
    1. Weaker
    2. Stayed about the same
    3. Stronger

V36 Party ID Summary
    0. Strong Democrat
    1. Weak Democrat
    2. Independent-Leaning Democratic
    3. Independent
    4. Independent-Leaning Republican
    5. Weak Republican
    6. Strong Republican

V37   Was Iraq war worth the cost
1. Worth it
2. Not worth it

V38   Iraq war increased or decreased threat of terrorism
1. Increased
2. Kept about the same
3. Decreased

V39   Govt assistance to Blacks scale: self-placement
1. Govt should help Blacks
2.
3.
4. Neutral
5.
6.
7. Blacks should help themselves

V40   Federal budget spending: Social Security
1. Increased
2. Kept about the same
3. Decreased

V41   Federal budget spending: public schools
1. Increased
2. Kept about the same
3. Decreased

V42   Federal budget spending: foreign aid
1. Increased
2. Kept about the same
3. Decreased

V43   Federal budget spending: aid to the poor
1. Increased
2. Kept about the same
3. Decreased

V44   Federal budget spending: border security
1. Increased
2. Kept about the same
3. Decreased

V45   Federal budget spending: war on terrorism
               1.   Increased
               2.   Kept about the same
               3.   Decreased

V46   Favor/oppose death penalty
               1.   Favor
               2.   Oppose

V47   Should fed govt make it more difficult to buy a gun
               1.   More difficult
               2.   Keep rules about the same/make it easier

V48   Black President makes R uncomfortable
               1.   Extremely uncomfortable
               2.   Very uncomfortable
               3.   Moderately uncomfortable
               4.   Slightly uncomfortable
               5.   Not uncomfortable at all

V49   Black President makes R pleased
               1.   Extremely Pleased
               2.   Very Pleased
               3.   Moderately Pleased
               4.   Slightly Pleased
               5.   Not Pleased at all

V50   Hope that U.S. has African-American President
               0.   No
               1.   Yes

V51   U.S. ready for African-American President
               0.   No
               1.   Yes

V52   U.S. more or less secure than when Pres took office
               1.   More secure
               2.   No change
               3.   Less secure

V53   Is religion important part of R life
               1.   Important
               2.   Not important

V54   Consider self born again
           1. Yes
           2. No

V55   Stereotype: Whites hard-working
           1. Hard-working
           2.
           3.
           4. Neutral
           5.
           6.
           7. Lazy

V56   Stereotype: Blacks hard-working
           1. Hard-working
           2.
           3.
           4. Neutral
           5.
           6.
           7. Lazy

V57   Stereotype: Whites intelligent
           1. Intelligent
           2.
           3.
           4. Neutral
           5.
           6.
           7. Unintelligent

V58   Stereotype: Blacks intelligent
           1. Intelligent
           2.
           3.
           4. Neutral
           5.
           6.
           7. Unintelligent

V59   Position on gay marriage
           1. Should be allowed
           2. Should not be allowed to marry but allow civil union, etc.
           3. Should not be allowed

V60   Marital status
                 1.   Married
                 2.   Divorced
                 3.   Separated
                 4.   Widowed
                 5.   Never married
                 6.   Partnered, not married {VOL}

V61   Highest grade of school or year of college completed
                 1.   < HS
                 2.   HS
                 3.   Some college, Associates, no Bachelor's
                 4.   Bachelor's degree
                 5.   > Bachelor's

V62   Household income (categories are the *numbers* 1–25)
                 1.   A. None or less than $2,999
                 2.   B. $3,000–$4,999
                 3.   C. $5,000–$7,499
                 4.   D. $7,500–$9,999
                 5.   E. $10,000–$10,999
                 6.   F. $11,000–$12,499
                 7.   G. $12,500–$14,999
                 8.   H. $15,000–$16,999
                 9.   J. $17,000–$19,999
                 10. K. $20,000–$21,999
                 11. M. $22,000–$24,999
                 12. N. $25,000–$29,999
                 13. P. $30,000–34,999
                 14. Q. $35,000–$39,999
                 15. R. $40,000–$44,999
                 16. S. $45,000–$49,999
                 17. T. $50,000–$59,999
                 18. U. $60,000–$74,999
                 19. V. $75,000–$89,999
                 20. W. $90,000–$99,999
                 21. X. $100,000–$109,999
                 22. Y. $110,000–$119,999
                 23. Z. $120,000–$134,999
                 24. AA. $135,000–$149,999
                 25. BB. $150,000 and over

POST-ELECTION INTERVIEW PHASE:

V63   How often trust the media to report news fairly
1. Just about always
2. Most of the time
3. Only some of the time
4. Almost never

V64   Did R vote in 2008 election
1. Nonvoter
2. Voter

V65   Did R vote on election day or before election day
1. Election day
2. Some time before this

V66   For whom did R vote for President
1. Barack Obama
2. John McCain

V67   NONVOTER: Who did R prefer for President
1. Barack Obama
2. John McCain

V68   Party of R's vote for House
1. Democratic candidate
2. Republican candidate

V69   SUMMARY: Party of R's vote for Senate*
1. Democratic candidate
2. Republican candidate

V70   PERSONAL OPTIMISM
1. Very optimistic
2. Somewhat optimistic
3. Lean toward being optimistic
4. Do not lean either way
5. Lean toward being pessimistic
6. Somewhat pessimistic
7. Very pessimistic

V71   Feeling thermometer: JOE BIDEN
        Mean = 58.0 Median = 60.0

V72   Feeling thermometer: SARAH PALIN
        Mean = 51.3 Median = 50.0

V73   Feeling thermometer: HISPANICS
Mean = 65.3 Median = 60.0

V74   Feeling thermometer: CHRISTIAN
FUNDAMENTALISTS   Mean= 56.3   Median = 50.0

*Note—roughly 2/3 of the states have a Senate race every electoral cycle. Responses from individuals in this subset may be somewhat different from those in the entire sample depending upon which states held Senate races in 2008.

V75   Feeling thermometer: LIBERALS
Mean = 54.7 Median = 50.0

V76   Feeling thermometer: CONSERVATIVES
Mean = 60.3 Median = 60.0

V77   Feeling thermometer: GAY MEN AND LESBIANS
Mean = 49.4 Median = 50.0

V78   Feeling thermometer: BLACKS
Mean = 68.8 Median = 70.0

V79   Feeling thermometer: ILLEGAL IMMIGRANTS
Mean = 39.4 Median = 40.0

V80   Feeling thermometer: WHITES
Mean = 73.0 Median = 70.0

V81   Feeling thermometer: MUSLIMS
Mean = 50.4 Median = 50.0

V82   Know party with most members in House before election
1. Democrats
2. DK
3. Republicans

V83   Know party with most members in Senate before election
1. Democrats
2. DK
3. Republicans

V84   U.S. policy goal: bring democracy to world
1. Very important
2. Somewhat important
3. Not important at all

V85   U.S. policy goal: control illegal immigration
1. Very important
2. Somewhat important
3. Not important at all

V86   U.S. policy goal: combat international terrorism
1. Very important
2. Somewhat important
3. Not important at all

V87   What should immigration levels be
1. Increased a lot
2. Increased a little
3. Left the same as it is now
4. Decreased a little
5. Decreased a lot

V88   How likely immigration take away jobs
1. Extremely likely
2. Very likely
3. Somewhat likely
4. Not at all likely

V89   Need strong govt for complex problems OR free market
1. Need a strong govt to handle complex economic problems
2. Free market can handle without govt involvement

V90   Hope the U.S. has a woman present in R's lifetime
1. Hope the U.S. has a woman President
2. Do not hope either way
3. Hope the U.S. does not have a woman President

V91   Important differences in what major parties stand for
1. Yes, differences
2. No, no differences

V92   Do women miss out on jobs because of discrimination
1. Agree strongly
2. Agree somewhat
3. Neither agree nor disagree
4. Disagree somewhat
5. Disagree strongly

V93   World is changing and we should adjust
1. Agree strongly
2. Agree somewhat

3. Neither agree nor disagree
4. Disagree somewhat
5. Disagree strongly

V94   Newer lifestyles breaking down society
1. Agree strongly
2. Agree somewhat
3. Neither agree nor disagree
4. Disagree somewhat
5. Disagree strongly

V95   Should be more tolerant of other moral standards
1. Agree strongly
2. Agree somewhat
3. Neither agree nor disagree
4. Disagree somewhat
5. Disagree strongly

V96   More emphasis on traditional family ties
1. Agree strongly
2. Agree somewhat
3. Neither agree nor disagree
4. Disagree somewhat
5. Disagree strongly

V97   Govt run by a few big interests or for benefit of all
1. Govt run by a few big interests
2. Govt run for the benefit of all

V98   Does government waste much tax money
1. Waste a lot
2. Waste some
3. Don't waste very much

V99   How many in government are crooked
1. Quite a few are crooked
2. Not very many are crooked
3. Hardly any are crooked

V100   R likes responsibility for handling a lot of thinking
1. Likes
2. Neither likes nor dislikes
3. Dislikes

V101   R prefers simple problems or complex problems
            1.   Simple
            2.   Complex

V102   Like-dislike: Democratic Party
            0.   Strongly dislike
            1.
            2.
            3.
            4.
            5.   Neutral
            6.
            7.
            8.
            9.
            10. Strongly like

V103   Like-dislike: Republican Party
            0.   Strongly dislike
            1.
            2.
            3.
            4.
            5.   Neutral
            6.
            7.
            8.
            9.
            10. Strongly like

V104   How satisfied is R with life
            1.   Extremely satisfied
            2.   Very satisfied
            3.   Moderately satisfied
            4.   Slightly satisfied
            5.   Not satisfied at all

A2: ANES2012 CODEBOOK

NOTE: Two data files are associated with this codebook.
    ANES2012A.SAV includes all of the following variables and all of the face-to-face (not web) survey respondents (N = 2054).
    ANES2012S.SAV includes only the variables whose names are in *italics*, and only those respondents who were interviewed face-to-face

(not web) and who claim to have voted in the general election for the House of Representatives (N = 1079).

This data set can be analyzed with the reduced, student version of **SPSS** and **SMALL STATA**.

Note that you will not be able to answer any questions about why someone voted (or not) as nonvoters have been eliminated.

Variable Name	Variable Label
	Value. Value Label
PW2012	SAMPLE WEIGHT—POST-ELECTION
	0. No Post-election interview
V1	GENDER
	1. Male
	2. Female
V2R	RACE
	1. White non-Hispanic
	2. Black non-Hispanic
	3. Hispanic
	4. Other non-Hispanic
V3	LATINO
	1. Latino
	2. Not Latino
V4	AGE (actual coded—based on year of birth)
	Mean = 47.25 Median = 47.0
	17. 17 years old
	18. 18 years old
	.
	.
	.
	90. 90 years old or older
V5	State postal code (e.g., AK = Alaska)
V8	Did R vote for President in 2008
	1. Yes, voted
	2. No, didn't vote

V9   Recall of last (2008) Presidential vote choice
1. Barack Obama
2. John McCain

V10   Approve/disapprove Pres handling job
1. Approve strongly
2. Approve not strongly
3. Neither/DK
4. Disapprove not strongly
5. Disapprove strongly

V11   Approve/disapprove Pres handling economy
1. Approve strongly
2. Approve not strongly
3. Neither/DK
4. Disapprove not strongly
5. Disapprove strongly

V12   Approve/disapprove Pres handling foreign relations
1. Approve strongly
2. Approve not strongly
3. Neither/DK
4. Disapprove not strongly
5. Disapprove strongly

V13   Approve/disapprove Pres handling health care
1. Approve strongly
2. Approve not strongly
3. Neither/DK
4. Disapprove not strongly
5. Disapprove strongly

V14   Approve/disapprove Pres handling war in Afghanistan
1. Approve strongly
2. Approve not strongly
3. Neither/DK
4. Disapprove not strongly
5. Disapprove strongly

I'd like to get your feelings toward some of our political leaders and other people who are in the news these days. I'll read the name of a person and I'd like you to rate that person using something we call the feeling thermometer. Ratings between 50 degrees and 100 degrees mean that you feel favorable and warm toward the person. Ratings between 0 degrees and 50 degrees mean that you don't feel favorable toward the person and that you don't care too much for that person. You would rate the person at the 50 degree mark if you don't feel particularly warm or cold toward the person. If we come to a person whose name you don't recognize, you don't need to rate that person. Just tell me and we'll move on to the next one.

V15	Feeling Thermometer: George W. Bush Mean = 46.0 Median = 50.0
V16	Feeling Thermometer: Democratic Presidential candidate Mean = 57.3 Median = 60.0
V17	Feeling Thermometer: Republican Presidential candidate Mean = 48.6 Median = 50.0
V18	Feeling Thermometer: Democratic Party Mean = 55.3 Median = 60.0
V19	Feeling Thermometer: Republican Party Mean = 47.2 Median = 50.0

V20   R better/worse off than 1 year ago
1. Better
2. The Same
3. Worse

V21   Will R be financially better/worse off one year from now
1. Better
2. The Same
3. Worse

V22   Does R have health insurance
1. Yes
2. No

V23   Affect for Democratic Pres candidate: angry
0. Yes
1. No

V24   Affect for Democratic Pres candidate: hopeful
0. No
1. Yes

V25   Affect for Democratic Pres candidate: afraid
0. Yes
1. No

V26   Affect for Democratic Pres candidate: proud
- 0. No
- 1. Yes

V27   Affect for Republican Pres candidate: angry
- 0. Yes
- 1. No

V28   Affect for Republican Pres candidate: hopeful
- 0. No
- 1. Yes

V29   Affect for Republican Pres candidate: afraid
- 0. Yes
- 1. No

V30   Affect for Republican Pres candidate: proud
- 0. No
- 1. Yes

V31   Will Pres race be close or will (winner) win by a lot
- 1. Will be close
- 2. Win by quite a bit

V32   Will Pres race be close in state
- 1. Will be close
- 2. Win by quite a bit

V33   Economy better worse in last year
- 1. Much better
- 2. Somewhat better
- 3. Stayed about the same
- 4. Somewhat worse
- 5. Much worse

V34   Which party better: handling nation's economy
- 1. Democrats
- 2. Either/Neither
- 3. Republicans

V35   During last year, U.S. position in world weaker/
stronger
- 1. Weaker
- 2. Stayed about the same
- 3. Stronger

V36	Party ID Summary
	0. Strong Democrat
	1. Weak Democrat
	2. Independent-Leaning Democratic
	3. Independent
	4. ILRIndependent-Leaning Republican
	5. Weak Republican
	6. Strong Republican

V37	Was Afghanistan war worth the cost
	1. Worth it
	2. Not worth it

V38	Afghanistan war increased or decreased threat of terrorism
	1. Increased
	2. Kept about the same
	3. Decreased

V38R	Approve/disapprove govt efforts to reduce terrorism
	1. Approve
	2. Neither approve/disapprove
	3. Disapprove

V38T	Favor or oppose torture for suspected terrorists
	1. Favor
	2. Neither favor/oppose
	3. Oppose

V39	Govt assistance to Blacks scale: self-placement
	1. Govt should help Blacks
	2.
	3.
	4. Neutral
	5.
	6.
	7. Blacks should help themselves

V40	Federal budget spending: Social Security
	1. Increased
	2. Kept about the same
	3. Decreased

V41	Federal budget spending: public schools
	1. Increased
	2. Kept about the same
	3. Decreased

V42E   Federal budget spending: the environment
            1. Increased
            2. Kept about the same
            3. Decreased

V43   Federal budget spending: aid to the poor
            1. Increased
            2. Kept about the same
            3. Decreased

V44S   Federal budget spending: science and technology
            1. Increased
            2. Kept about the same
            3. Decreased

V45S   Federal budget spending: child care
            1. Increased
            2. Kept about the same
            3. Decreased

V46   Favor/oppose death penalty
            1. Favor
            2. Oppose

V47   Should fed govt make it more difficult to buy a gun
            1. More difficult
            2. Keep rules about the same/make it easier

V48T   Do you support, oppose, or neither support nor oppose
            the Tea Party movement?
            1. Support
            2. Neither support nor oppose
            3. Oppose

V52   U.S. more or less secure than when Pres took office
            1. More secure
            2. No change
            3. Less secure

V53   Is religion important part of R life
            1. Important
            2. Not important

V54   Consider self born again
            1. Yes
            2. No

V55   Stereotype: Whites hardworking
    1. Hard-working
    2.
    3.
    4. Neutral
    5.
    6.
    7. Lazy

V56   Stereotype: Blacks hardworking
    1. Hard-working
    2.
    3.
    4. Neutral
    5.
    6.
    7. Lazy

V57   Stereotype: Whites intelligent
    1. Intelligent
    2.
    3.
    4. Neutral
    5.
    6.
    7. Unintelligent

V58   Stereotype: Blacks intelligent
    1. Intelligent
    2.
    3.
    4. Neutral
    5.
    6.
    7. Unintelligent

V59   Position on gay marriage
    1. Should be allowed
    2. Should not be allowed to marry but allow civil union, etc.
    3. Should not be allowed

V60   Marital status
    1. Married
    2. Divorced
    3. Separated

4. Widowed
5. Never married
6. Partnered, not married {VOL}

V61   Highest grade of school or year of college completed
1. < HS
2. HS
3. Some college, Associates, no Bachelor's
4. Bachelor's degree
5. > Bachelor's

V62A   Household income (categories are the *numbers* 1–28)
01. Under $5,000
02. $5,000–$9,999
03. $10,000–$12,499
04. $12,500–$14,999
05. $15,000–$17,499
06. $17,500–$19,999
07. $20,000–$22,499
08. $22,500–$24,999
09. $25,000–$27,499
10. $27,500–$29,999
11. $30,000–$34,999
12. $35,000–$39,999
13. $40,000–$44,999
14. $45,000–$49,999
15. $50,000–$54,999
16. $55,000–$59,999
17. $60,000–$64,999
18. $65,000–$69,999
19. $70,000–$74,999
20. $75,000–$79,999
21. $80,000–$89,999
22. $90,000–$99,999
23. $100,000–$109,999
24. $110,000–$124,999
25. $125,000–$149,999
26. $150,000–$174,999
27. $175,000–$249,999
28. $250,000 or more

V63J   Electoral integrity: is journalist coverage fair
1. Very often
2. Fairly often
3. Not often
4. Not at all often

V63T   Does federal govt pose a threat to citizens
                1. Yes
                2. No

V63R   Electoral integrity: do the rich buy elections
                1. Very often
                2. Fairly often
                3. Not often
                4. Not at all often

POST-ELECTION INTERVIEW PHASE:
V64   Did R vote in 2012 election
                1. Nonvoter
                2. Voter

V66   For whom did R vote for President
                1. Barack Obama
                2. W. Mitt Romney

V68   Party of R's vote for House
                1. Democratic candidate
                2. Republican candidate

V69   SUMMARY: Party of R's vote for Senate*
                1. Democratic candidate
                2. Republican candidate

*Note—roughly 2/3 of the states have a Senate race every electoral cycle. Responses from individuals in this subset may be somewhat different from those in the entire sample depending upon which states held Senate races in 2012.

V71   Feeling thermometer: JOE BIDEN
                Mean = 54.0 Median = 50.0

V72   Feeling thermometer: PAUL RYAN
                Mean = 51.2 Median = 50.0

V74   Feeling thermometer: CHRISTIAN
                FUNDAMENTALISTS
                Mean = 53.4 Median = 50.0

V75   Feeling thermometer: LIBERALS
                Mean = 52.1 Median = 50.0

V75B	Feeling thermometer: BIG BUSINESS
	Mean = 53.4 Median = 50.0

V76	Feeling thermometer: CONSERVATIVES
	Mean = 57.7 Median = 60.0

V77	Feeling thermometer: GAY MEN AND LESBIANS
	Mean = 53.7 Median = 50.0

V78	Feeling thermometer: BLACKS
	Mean = 66.3 Median = 70.0

V79	Feeling thermometer: ILLEGAL IMMIGRANTS
	Mean = 40.0 Median = 40.0

V80	Feeling thermometer: WHITES
	Mean = 72.5 Median = 70.0

V81	Feeling thermometer: MUSLIMS
	Mean = 47.9 Median = 50.0

V81M	Feeling thermometer: MORMONS
	Mean = 52.5 Median = 50.0

V81R	Feeling Thermometer: RICH PEOPLE
	Mean = 54.3 Median = 50

V81T	Feeling thermometer: TEA PARTY
	Mean = 46.2 Median = 50.0

V82   Know party with most members in House before
        election
        1. Democrats
        2. DK
        3. Republicans

V83   Know party with most members in Senate before
        election
        1. Democrats
        2. DK
        3. Republicans

V87   What should immigration levels be
        1. Increased a lot
        2. Increased a little
        3. Left the same as it is now
        4. Decreased a little
        5. Decreased a lot

V88   How likely immigration take away jobs
1. Extremely likely
2. Very likely
3. Somewhat likely
4. Not at all likely

V88P   U.S. government policy toward unauthorized immigrants
1. Make all unauthorized immigrants felons and send them back to their home country
2. Have a guest worker program that allows unauthorized immigrants to remain
3. Allow unauthorized immigrants to remain in the United States . . . certain requirements
4. Allow unauthorized immigrants to remain in the United States . . . without penalties

V88C   Allow citizenship to some illegal aliens
1. Favor
2. Neither favor/oppose
3. Oppose

V89   Need strong govt for complex problems OR free market
1. Need a strong govt to handle complex economic problems
2. Free market can handle without govt involvement

V90W   Woman president in next 20 years—good or bad
1. Good
2. Neither good/bad
3. Bad

V91   Important differences in what major parties stand for
1. Yes, differences
2. No, no differences

V92H   Discrimination against women
1. Not a problem at all
2. A minor problem
3. A moderately serious problem
4. A very serious problem
5. An extremely serious problem

V93   World is changing and we should adjust
     1.   Agree strongly
     2.   Agree somewhat
     3.   Neither agree nor disagree
     4.   Disagree somewhat
     5.   Disagree strongly

V94   Newer lifestyles breaking down society
     1.   Agree strongly
     2.   Agree somewhat
     3.   Neither agree nor disagree
     4.   Disagree somewhat
     5.   Disagree strongly

V95   Should be more tolerant of other moral standards
     1.   Agree strongly
     2.   Agree Somewhat
     3.   Neither agree nor disagree
     4.   Disagree somewhat
     5.   Disagree strongly

V96   More emphasis on traditional family ties
     1.   Agree strongly
     2.   Agree somewhat
     3.   Neither agree nor disagree
     4.   Disagree somewhat
     5.   Disagree strongly

V97   Govt run by a few big interests or for benefit of all
     1.   Govt run by a few big interests
     5.   Govt run for the benefit of all

V98   Does government waste much tax money. Note:
     pre-election
     1.   Waste a lot
     2.   Waste some
     3.   Don't waste very much

V99C   How many in government are corrupt
     1.   All
     2.   Most
     3.   About half
     4.   A few
     5.   None

V99P	How often can people be trusted

1. Always
2. Most of the time
3. About half of the time
4. Some of the time
5. Never

V99E	Elections make govt pay attention

1. A good deal
2. Some
3. Not much

V99D	Makes a difference whom one votes for

1. Won't make a difference
2.
3.
4.
5. Can make a big difference

V102	Like-dislike: Democratic Party

0. Strongly dislike
1.
2.
3.
4.
5. Neutral
6.
7.
8.
9.
10. Strongly like

V103	Like-dislike: Republican Party

0. Strongly dislike
1.
2.
3.
4.
5. Neutral
6.
7.
8.
9.
10. Strongly like

V104   How satisfied is R with life
1.   Extremely satisfied
2.   Very satisfied
3.   Moderately satisfied
4.   Slightly satisfied
5.   Not satisfied at all

V105   Is global warming happening or not
1.   Has probably been happening
2.   Probably hasn't been happening

V106   7-point scale liberal/conservative self-placement.
Note: pre-election
1.   Extremely liberal
2.   Liberal
3.   Slightly liberal
4.   Moderate/middle of the road
5.   Slightly conservative
6.   Conservative
7.   Extremely conservative
-1.   Haven't thought much about this

A3: CONGRESS2008 CODEBOOK

Variable Name	Variable Label Value. Value Label
STATE	ANES POSTAL CODE ABBREVIATION
STATENO	Number of state if listed alphabetically
CD	Congressional District Number
MEMBER	Name of district winner
INC08	Incumbency status of election[1]

INC08
1.   Democratic incumbent
2.   Republican incumbent
3.   Open seat-previously held by Democrat
4.   Open seat-previously held by Republican

PARTY08   Winning Party 2008
1.   Democratic
2.   Republican

DHV08	Percentage won by Democratic candidate
RHV08	Percentage won by Republican candidate
WV08	Percentage won by winning candidate

		National[2]
OBAMA	District's vote for Obama[3]	52.93%
McCAIN	District vote for McCain	45.65%
KERRY	District vote for Kerry (2004)	48.27%
BUSH	District vote for Bush (2004)	50.73%
DH$08	Expenditures for Democratic House candidate[4]	
RH$08	Expenditures for Republican House candidate	
SENIORITY08	Number of years served by incumbent	
PU08	Party Unity Score 2008[5]	
PU09	Party Unity Score 2009	
PS08A	Presidential Support Score All[6]	
PS08N	Presidential Support Score Non-unanimous Votes Only	
ACU08	American Conservative Union Rating 2008[7]	
ACU09	American Conservative Union Rating 2009	
DWNOM110	DW-NOMINATE SCORE 110th Congress[8]	
DWNOM111	DW-NOMINATE SCORE 111th Congress	

		National[2]
TOTPOP	Total population estimate for district[9]	685,453
MEDIANAGE	Median age of district resident	36.40
WHITE	Percentage Whites in district	74.13%
BLACK	Percentage Blacks in district	12.37%
HISPANIC	Percentage Hispanic in District	14.73%
PER65	Percentage 65 and older	12.47%
LT18	Percentage under 18	25.00%
COLLEGE	Percentage 25 years or older completing college or advanced degree	27.00%
PCI	Per capita income	$26,178
MV	Median value of owner-occupied dwelling	$181,800
MHI	Median household income	$50,007
HGINI	Gini index based on households (measure of income inequality)[10]	.465
MFI	Median family income	$60,374
VET18	Percentage of those 18 and over who are veterans (male and female)	10.44%

▌ NOTES AND SOURCES

1   To avoid confusion when using certain variables (**SENIORITY08, PU08, PS08A, PS08N, ACU08, DWNOMINATE110**), data were eliminated for those members of Congress who did not run for reelection in the general election (a few were eliminated in primaries). These correspond to **INC08** categories 3 and 4.

2 Other than **TOTPOP**, these figures will not necessarily be exactly the same as the means calculated from the 435 districts. Why? By 2005–07, districts were not of equal population size. They each, therefore, carry different weight in the calculation of the true population figures. These figures also include Washington, D.C., and Puerto Rico, both of which have no House representation (other than a delegate).

3 Presidential vote by district: http://www.swingstateproject.com/showDiary. do?diaryId=4161.

   Presidential vote 2008—national: http://www.fec.gov/pubrec/fe2008/tables 2008.pdf.

   Presidential vote 2004—national: http://www.fec.gov/pubrec/fe2008/tables 2008.pdf.

4 Finance data: http://fec.gov/DisclosureSearch/mapHSApp.do?election_ yr=2008.

5 Party unity scores courtesy of Keith Poole.

6 Presidential support scores courtesy of George C. Edwards III. Unlike the standard CQ support scores, Dr. Edwards, among other modifications, includes paired votes in each member's calculation. The first score represents the proportion of times that a member sided with the president on all roll call votes upon which President Bush had declared a position. The second only includes those roll call votes that were non-unanimous. The latter will increase the mean difference between Democrats and Republicans.

7 American Conservative Union scores:

   http://www.conservative.org/ratings/ratingsarchive/2008/2008house.htm

   http://www.conservative.org/ratings/ratingsarchive/2009/House Ratings.htm

8 Description: Based upon a multidimensional scaling of roll calls, House members are ranked from most liberal (negative score) to most conservative (positive score). Only the first dimension, corresponding to economic issues, is used. Scores courtesy of Keith Poole.

   DWNOM110: Legislator's **DW-NOMINATE** score for the 110th Congress (2007–2008), 1st dimension only (from http://www.voteview. com/dwnomin.htm; Legislator Estimates 1st to 111th Houses Excel file)

   DWNOM111: Legislator's **DW-NOMINATE** score for the 111th Congress (2009–2010), 1st dimension only (from http://www.voteview. com/dwnomin.htm; Legislator Estimates 1st to 111th Houses Excel file)

9 Demographic data: 2005–2007 American Community Survey 3-Year Estimates.

   http://factfinder.census.gov/servlet/GCTGeoSearchByListServlet?ds_ name=ACS_2007_3YR_G00_&_lang=en&_ts=320436047885.

10 Based on the Lorenz curve, a score of 0.0 means perfect equality of household incomes, 1.00 perfect inequality. It corresponds to the area between the Lorenz income distribution curve and the line of perfect equality.

A4: CONGRESS2008–2012 CODEBOOK

(Not suitable for the Student Version of SPSS nor SMALL STATA.)

Variable Name	Variable Label Value. Value Label
STATE	ANES Postal Code Abbreviation
STATENO	Number of State if Listed Alphabetically
CD08	Congressional District Number 2008–2010 elections
CD12	Congressional District Number 2012
MEMBER08	Name of district winner 2008
MEMBER10	Name of district winner 2010
MEMBER12	Name of district winner 2012
INC08	Incumbency status of 2008 election[1]
INC10	Incumbency status of 2010 election
INC12	Incumbency status of 2012 election
	1. Democratic incumbent
	2. Republican Incumbent
	3. Open seat-previously held by Democrat
	4. Open seat-previously held by Republican
PARTY08	Winning Party 2008
PARTY10	Winning Party 2010
PARTY12	Winning Party 2012
	1. Democratic
	2. Republican
DHV08	Percentage won by Democratic candidate in 2008 (of all votes)[1]
DHV10	Percentage won by Democratic candidate in 2010
DHV12	Percentage won by Democratic candidate in 2012
RHV08	Percentage won by Republican candidate in 2008
RHV10	Percentage won by Republican candidate in 2010
RHV12	Percentage won by Republican candidate in 2012
WV08	Percentage won by winning candidate in 2008
WV10	Percentage won by winning candidate in 2010
WV12	Percentage won by winning candidate in 2012
OBAMA08	District's 2008 vote for Obama, 2008–2010 districts[2]
OBAMA08A	District's 2008 vote for Obama, 2012 districts
OBAMA2012	Districts 2012 vote for Obama (only use with 2012 data)
McCAIN08	District's 2008 vote for McCain, 2008–2010 districts
McCAIN08A	District's 2012 vote for McCain, 2012 districts
ROMNEY2012	District's 2012 vote for Romney, 2012 districts (only use with 2012 data)

KERRY04	District vote for Kerry (2004) (only use with 2008–2010 data)
BUSH04	District vote for Bush (2004) (only use with 2008–2010 data)
DH$08	2008 Expenditures for Democratic House candidate[3]
DH$10	2010 Expenditures for Democratic House candidate
DH$12	2012 Expenditures for Democratic House candidate
RH$08	2008 Expenditures for Republican House candidate
RH$10	2010 Expenditures for Republican House candidate
RH$12	2012 Expenditures for Republican House candidate
DHC08	2008 Total Contributions to Democratic House candidate
DHC10	2010 Total Contributions to Democratic House candidate
DHC12	2012 Total Contributions to Democratic House candidate
RHC08	2008 Total Contributions to Republican House candidate
RHC10	2010 Total Contributions to Republican House candidate
RHC12	2012 Total Contributions to Republican House candidate
DHIND08	2008 Total Contributions to Democratic candidate from individuals
DHIND10	2010 Total Contributions to Democratic candidate from individuals
DHIND12	2012 Total Contributions to Democratic candidate from individuals
RHIND08	2008 Total Contributions to Republican candidate from individuals
RHIND10	2010 Total Contributions to Republican candidate from individuals
RHIND12	2012 Total Contributions to Republican candidate from individuals
DHIND08A	2008 Total Contributions ≤ $200 to Democratic candidate from individuals
DHIND10A	2010 Total Contributions ≤ $200 tor Democratic candidate from individuals
DHIND12A	2012 Total Contributions ≤ $200 to Democratic candidate from individuals
RHIND08A	2008 Total Contributions ≤ $200 to Republican candidate from individuals
RHIND10A	2010 Total Contributions ≤ $200 to Republican candidate from individuals
RHIND12A	2012 Total Contributions ≤ $200 to Republican candidate from individuals
DHP08	2008 Total Contributions to Democratic candidate from party committees
DHP10	2010 Total Contributions to Democratic candidate from party committees

DHP12	2012 Total Contributions to Democratic candidate from party committees
RHP08	2008 Total Contributions to Republican candidate from party committees
RHP10	2010 Total Contributions to Republican candidate from party committees
RHP12	2012 Total Contributions to Republican candidate from party committees
DHO08	2008 Total Contributions to Democratic candidate from other committees, mainly PACs
DHO10	2010 Total Contributions to Democratic candidate from other committees, mainly PACs
DHO12	2012 Total Contributions to Democratic candidate from other committees, mainly PACs
RHO08	2008 Total Contributions to Republican candidate from other committees, mainly PACs
RHO10	2010 Total Contributions to Republican candidate from other committees, mainly PACs
RHO12	2012 Total Contributions to Republican candidate from other committees, mainly PACs
SENIORITY08	Number of years served by incumbent in 2008
SENIORITY10	Number of years served by incumbent in 2010
SENIORITY12	Number of years served by incumbent in 2012
SENIORITY14	Number of years served by incumbent in 2014
PU08	Party Unity Score 2008[4]
PU09	Party Unity Score 2009
PU10	Party Unity Score 2010
PU11	Party Unity Score 2011
PU12	Party Unity Score 2012
PS08A	Presidential Support Score All, 2008[5]
PS09A	Presidential Support Score All, 2009
PS10A	Presidential Support Score All, 2010
PS11A	Presidential Support Score All, 2011
PS12A	Presidential Support Score All, 2012
PS08N	Presidential Support Score Non-unanimous Votes Only, 2008
PS09N	Presidential Support Score Non-unanimous Votes Only, 2009
PS10N	Presidential Support Score Non-unanimous Votes Only, 2010
PS11N	Presidential Support Score Non-unanimous Votes Only, 2011
PS12N	Presidential Support Score Non-unanimous Votes Only, 2012

ACU08	American Conservative Union Rating 2008[6]
ACU09	American Conservative Union Rating 2009
ACU10	American Conservative Union Rating 2010
ACU11	American Conservative Union Rating 2011
ACU12	American Conservative Union Rating 2012
ACU13	American Conservative Union Rating 2013
DWNOM110	DW-NOMINATE SCORE 110th Congress[7]
DWNOM111	DW-NOMINATE SCORE 111th Congress
DWNOM112	DW-NOMINATE SCORE 112th Congress
TOTPOP08	Total population estimate for district[8]
MEDIANAGE08	Median age of district resident
WHITE08	Percentage Whites in district
BLACK08	Percentage Blacks in district
HISPANIC08	Percentage Hispanic in district
PER6508	Percentage 65 and older
LT1808	Percentage under 18
COLLEGE08	Percentage 25 years or older completing college or advanced degree
PCI08	Per capita income
MV08	Median value of owner-occupied dwelling
MHI08	Median household income
MFI08	Median family income
VET1808	Percentage of those 18 and over who are veterans (male and female)
TOTPOP10	Total population estimate for district
MEDIANAGE10	Median age of district resident
WHITE10	Percentage Whites in district
BLACK10	Percentage Blacks in district
HISPANIC10	Percentage Hispanic in district
PER6510	Percentage 65 and older
LT1810	Percentage under 18
COLLEGE10	Percentage 25 years or older completing college or advanced degree
PCI10	Per capita income
MV10	Median value of owner-occupied dwelling
MHI10	Median household income
MFI10	Median family income
VET1810	Percentage of those 18 and over
TOTPOP12	Total population estimate for district
MEDIANAGE12	Median age of district resident
WHITE12	Percentage Whites in district
BLACK12	Percentage Blacks in district
HISPANIC12	Percentage Hispanic in district
PER6512	Percentage 65 and older

LT1812	Percentage under 18
COLLEGE12	Percentage 25 years or older completing college or advanced degree
PCI12	Per capita income
MV12	Median value of owner-occupied dwelling
MHI12	Median household income
MFI12	Median family income
VET1812	Percentage of those 18 and over who are veterans (male and female)

NOTES AND SOURCES

1   All percentages are of total votes cast, not just two party. To obtain the percentage of the two-party vote (within rounding error), divide DHV/(DHV + RHV), etc. When two candidates of the same party (CA in 2012 and LA) ran against each other, these data were eliminated.

2   Presidential vote by district:

   http://www.swingstateproject.com/showDiary.do?diaryId=4161
   http://www.dailykos.com/story/2012/11/19/1163009/-Daily-Kos-Elections-presidential-results-by-congressional-district-for-the-2012–2008-elections
   Presidential vote 2008—national: http://www.fec.gov/pubrec/fe2008/tables2008.pdf
   Presidential vote 2004—national: http://www.fec.gov/pubrec/fe2004/tables.pdf

3   Finance data: http://fec.gov/DisclosureSearch/mapHSApp.do?election_yr=2008, 2010, 2012.

4   Party unity scores courtesy of Keith Poole.

5   Presidential support scores courtesy of George C. Edwards III. Unlike the standard CQ support scores, Dr. Edwards, among other modifications, includes paired votes in each member's calculation. The first score represents the proportion of times that a member sided with the president on all roll call votes upon which President Bush had declared a position. The second only includes those roll call votes that were non-unanimous. The latter will increase the mean difference between Democrats and Republicans.

6   American Conservative Union scores:

   http://conservative.org/ratingsarchive/uscongress/2009, http://conservative.org/ratingsarchive/uscongress/2010, http://conservative.org/ratingsarchive/uscongress/2011, and http://conservative.org/ratingsarchive/uscongress/2012

7   Description: Based upon a multidimensional scaling of roll calls, House members are ranked from most liberal (negative score) to most conservative (positive score). Only the first dimension, corresponding to economic issues, is used. Scores courtesy of Keith Poole.

   Legislator Estimates 1st to 112th Houses: http://www.voteview.com/dwnomin.htm

8   Demographic data: 2006–2008 American Community Survey 3-Year Estimates:

2008–2010 American Community Survey 3-Year Estimates
2010–2012 American Community Survey 3-Year Estimates
2010–2012 ACS should only be used for the 113th Congress
The Census Bureau recommends only making comparisons with non-overlapping 3-year estimates. Therefore, one is cautioned to only compare the 2006–2008 with the 2010–2012 data.
Source: http://factfinder2.census.gov

A5: EUROBAROMETER 69:2 CODEBOOK

NOTE: Four data files are associated with this codebook.

EURO69.SAV includes all of the survey respondents (N = 26,661) from the 27 EU nations (March–May 2008). Northern Ireland and East Germany were sampled separately.
Respondents who were part of the split sample question file were eliminated.
Weight variable W27 should be used as it adjusts for different country populations.
The following data sets can be analyzed with the reduced, student version of **SPSS** and **SMALL STATA**.
Weight variable W1 should be used with each.
EURO69I.SAV includes only respondents from Italy (N = 1022).
EURO69H.SAV includes only respondents from Hungary (N = 1000)
EURO69D.SAV includes only respondents from Denmark (N = 1005)

Variable Name	Variable Label Value. Value Label
COUNTRY	Numerical Country Code[1]

1. Belgium	11. Luxembourg	21. Hungary
2. Denmark	12. Netherlands	22. Latvia
3. Germany (west)	13. Austria	23. Lithuania
4. Germany (east)	14. Portugal	24. Malta
5. Greece	15. Sweden	25. Poland
6. Spain	16. Great Britain	26. Slovakia
7. Finland	17. Northern Ireland	27. Slovenia
8. France	18. Cyprus	28. Bulgaria
9. Ireland	19. Czech Republic	29. Romania
10. Italy	20. Estonia	

W1   WEIGHT ADJUSTS FOR DEMOGRAPHIC INEQUALITIES IN SAMPLING FOR INDIVIDUAL COUNTRIES (only use with single country subsets or when comparing individual countries with each other)

W27   W1 PLUS ADJUSTMENT FOR COUNTRY POPULATIONS (27 EU member nations existing at the time. Use when analyzing the entire EU)

V1   QA3 LIFE SATISFACTION[2]
1. Very satisfied
2. Fairly satisfied
3. Not very satisfied
4. Not at all satisfied
5. Don't know[3] (.5%)

V2   QA4A EXPECTATIONS NEXT 12 MONTHS: LIFE IN GENERAL
1. Better
2. Same
3. Worse

V3   QA4A EXPECTATIONS N12M: ECONOMIC SITUATION IN YOUR COUNTRY
1. Better
2. Same
3. Worse

V4   QA4A EXPECTATIONS N12M: FINANCIAL SITUATION OF YOUR HOUSEHOLD
1. Better
2. Same
3. Worse

V5   QA4A EXPECTATIONS N12M: EMPLOYMENT SITUATION IN YOUR COUNTRY
1. Better
2. Same
3. Worse

V6   QA7A COUNTRY'S EU MEMBERSHIP—GOOD/BAD
1. A good thing
2. Neither good nor bad
3. A bad thing

V7   QA8A EU MEMBERSHIP—COUNTRY
BENEFITED FROM
1. Benefited
2. Not benefited

V8   QA11A PRESENT DIRECTION—COUNTRY
1. Going in the right direction
2. Neither/Don't know
3. Going in the wrong direction

V9   QA11A PRESENT DIRECTION—EUROPEAN
UNION
1. Going in the right direction
2. Neither (volunteered)/Don't know
3. Going in the wrong direction

V10   QA14 EU MEANING: LOSS OF CULTURAL
IDENTITY
0. Not mentioned
1. Mentioned

V11   QA15A EU STATEMENTS: PERSONAL VOICE
COUNTS IN EU
1. Tend to agree
2. DK
3. Tend to disagree

V12   QA15A EU STATEMENTS: PERSONAL VOICE
COUNTS IN COUNTRY
1. Tend to agree
2. DK
3. Tend to disagree

V13   QA15A EU STATEMENTS: MY COUNTRY'S
VOICE COUNTS IN EU
1. Tend to agree
2. DK
3. Tend to disagree

V14   QA27 HOUSEHOLD PURCHASING POWER—
LAST 5 YEARS
1. Improved
2. Stayed about the same
3. Got worse

V15   QA29 LIFE FOR THE NEXT GENERATION WILL BE
1. Easier
2. More difficult
3. Neither

V16   QA37 EU PROPOSALS: SINGLE CURRENCY FOR ALL COUNTRIES IN EU
1. For
2. DK
3. Against

V17   QA37 EU PROPOSALS: A COMMON FOREIGN POLICY AMONG ALL EU COUNTRIES
1. For
2. DK
3. Against

V18   QA37 EU PROPOSALS: A COMMON DEFENCE AND SECURITY POLICY AMONG ALL EU COUNTRIES
1. For
2. DK
3. Against

V19   QA47A GLOBALISATION IS AN OPPORTUNITY FOR ECONOMIC GROWTH
1. Strongly agree
2. Somewhat agree
3. DK
4. Somewhat disagree
5. Strongly disagree

V20   QA47A GLOBALISATION PRESENTS A THREAT TO OUR NATIONAL CULTURE
1. Strongly agree
2. Somewhat agree
3. DK
4. Somewhat disagree
5. Strongly disagree

V21   QC2 EUROPEAN ELECTIONS IN 2009—INTEREST
1. Very interested
2. Somewhat interested
3. Somewhat disinterested
4. Very disinterested

V22   QC3 EUROPEAN ELECTIONS—INTENTION
       TO VOTE (10-point scale)
       1. Definitely will not vote
       2.
       3.
       4.
       5.
       6.
       7.
       8.
       9.
       10. Definitely will vote

V23   QD1A IMMIGRANTS CONTRIBUTE A LOT TO
       OUR COUNTRY
       1. Totally agree
       2. Tend to agree
       3. DK
       4. Tend to disagree
       5. Totally disagree

V24   QE2T GLOBAL WARMING/CLIMATE
       CHANGE—PERCEPTION (10-point scale)
       1. Not a serious problem at all
       2.
       3.
       4.
       5.
       6.
       7.
       8.
       9.
       10. An extremely serious problem

V25   D1 LEFT-RIGHT IDEOLOGICAL PLACEMENT
       (10-point scale)
       1. Left
       2.
       3.
       4.
       5.
       6.

7.

8.

9.

10.   Right

11.   Refused to answer (8.3%)

12.   DK (11.1%)

V26   D7 MARITAL STATUS
1.   Married
2.   Remarried
3.   Unmarried, living with partner
4.   Unmarried, have never lived with partner
5.   Unmarried, previously lived with partner
6.   Divorced
7.   Separated
8.   Widowed

V27   D10 SEX
1.   Male
2.   Female

V28   D11 AGE (actual years coded: W27
WEIGHT)   Mean = 46.1 Median = 45.0
15.   Fifteen years old
16.
.
.
.

98.   Ninety eight years old

V29   D25 TYPE OF COMMUNITY
1.   Rural area or village
2.   Small or middle sized town
3.   Large town

V30   D41 NATIONAL BACKGROUND:
RESPONDENT WAS BORN
1.   In current country
2.   In another EU country
3.   In Europe, but not in the EU
4.   In Asia, Africa, or Latin America
5.   In Northern America, Japan, or Oceana

V31   D42 NATIONAL BACKGROUND: PARENTS
1.   Both parents born in current country
2.   One in current country, one in another EU country

3. Both in another EU country
4. One in current country, one outside of the EU
5. One in another EU country, one outside of EU
6. Refused to answer/DK (.2%)

NOTES

1 Country codes can be used to create aggregated or country-specific variables. For example, a variable listing the type of electoral system that a country has can be added. Here are the specific possibilities:

Single Member District/Winner Take All

First past the post: Great Britain (including Northern Ireland)
Two-round: France
Single Transferable Vote: Ireland, Malta

Mixed (combination of proportional and single-member district)

Mixed member: Germany (both), Hungary
Parallel: Lithuania

Proportional Representation-List: all others
Source: The International Institute for Democracy and Electoral Assistance http://www.idea.int/esd/glossary.cfm#N

2 Question code (e.g., QA3) corresponds to original survey entry.
3 "Don't Know" was included in most issue items as it often is the response of a sizeable proportion of the sample, sometimes exceeding 15%. They have been added to or included as a middle category. You may wish to eliminate these respondents by recoding their category to **SYSMIS** (**RECODE**, Form 1.1)

A6: CCES2012 CODEBOOK

NOTE: Three data files are associated with this codebook.

CCES2012.SAV includes all of the following variables and all of the survey respondents (N = 54,535).

CCES2012I.SAV includes only the variables whose names are in *italics*, and only those respondents from Indiana (N = 1,020) . This data set can be analyzed with the reduced, student version of **SPSS** and **SMALL STATA**.

CCES2012M.SAV includes only the variables whose names are in *italics*, and only those respondents from Maryland (N = 1,062) . This data set can be analyzed with the reduced, student version of **SPSS** and **SMALL STATA.**

WEIGHT	Common Content Weight
STATE	STATE NUMBER (listed at end of codebook)
CD112	Congressional District Number, 112th Congress
CD113	Congressional District Number, 113th Congress

V1   GENDER
1. Male
2. Female

V2   EDUCATION
1. No HS
2. High school graduate
3. Some college
4. 2-year
5. 4-year
6. Post-grad

V3   RACE/ETHNICITY (self best description)
1. White
2. Black
3. Hispanic
4. Asian
5. Native American
6. Mixed
7. Middle Eastern
8. Other

V4   HISPANIC
1. Yes
2. No

V5   AGE (based upon birth year)

V6   MARITAL STATUS
1. Married
2. Separated
3. Divorced
4. Widowed
5. Single
6. Domestic partnership

V7   REGISTERED (to vote)
1. Yes
2. No

V8   PARTY ID
1. Strong Democrat
2. Not very strong Democrat
3. Lean Democrat
4. Independent
5. Lean Republican
6. Not very strong Republican
7. Strong Republican

V9   BORN AGAIN: Would you describe yourself as a born-again or Evangelical Christian
1. Yes
2. No

V10   How important is religion in your life
1. Very important
2. Somewhat important
3. Not too important
4. Not at all important

V11   How often do you attend religious services
1. More than once a week
2. Once a week
3. Once or twice a month
4. A few times a year
5. Seldom
6. Never

V12   Present religion is
1. Protestant
2. Roman Catholic
3. Mormon
4. Eastern or Greek Orthodox
5. Jewish
6. Muslim
7. Buddhist
8. Hindu
9. Atheist
10. Agnostic
11. Nothing in particular
12. Something else

V13 Children under 18
1. Yes
2. No

V14 Do you follow what's going on in government and public affairs
1. Most of the time
2. Some of the time
3. Only now and then
4. Hardly at all

V15 Family income over past year
1. Less than $10,000
2. $10,000–$19,999
3. $20,000–$29,999
4. $30,000–$39,999
5. $40,000–$49,999
6. $50,000–$59,999
7. $60,000–$69,999
8. $70,000–$79,999
9. $80,000–$99,999
10. $100,000–$119,999
11. $120,000–$149,999
12. $150,000–$199,999
13. $200,000–$249,999
14. $250,000–$349,999
15. $350,000–$499,999
16. $500,000 or more

V16 Do you own or rent?
1. Own
2. Rent
3. Other

V17 You or immediate family member serve/served in military
1. Yes
2. No

V18 Immigrant/Citizen Status
1. Immigrant Citizen
2. Immigrant non-Citizen
3. First generation
4. Second
5. Third

V19   General health is
            1.   Excellent
            2.   Very good
            3.   Good
            4.   Fair
            5.   Poor

V20   Do you have health insurance?
            1.   Yes
            2.   No/Not Sure

V21   In the past 12 months, did you not see a doctor
            because of costs?
            1.   Yes
            2.   No

V22   Over the past year, the nation's economy has
            1.   Gotten much better
            2.   Gotten better
            3.   Stayed about the same
            4.   Gotten worse
            5.   Gotten much worse

V23   Over the past four years, your household annual
            income
            1.   Increased a lot
            2.   Increased somewhat
            3.   Stayed about the same
            4.   Decreased somewhat
            5.   Decreased a lot

V24   Over the next year, the nation's economy will
            1.   Get much better
            2.   Get somewhat better
            3.   Stay about the same
            4.   Get somewhat worse
            5.   Get much worse

V25   Who bears most responsibility for the current state of
            the U.S. economy?
            1.   Barack Obama
            2.   George W. Bush
            3.   Wall Street
            4.   World Economy
            5.   Congress

V26   Mistake to attack Iraq?
1. Yes
2. Not Sure
3. No

V27   Mistake to attack Afghanistan?
1. Yes
2. Not Sure
3. No

V28   Approval of Obama
1. Strongly Approve
2. Somewhat Approve
3. Somewhat Disapprove
4. Strongly Disapprove

V29   Approval of Congress
1. Strongly Approve
2. Somewhat Approve
3. Somewhat Disapprove
4. Strongly Disapprove

V30   Approval of U.S. House member
1. Strongly Approve
2. Somewhat Approve
3. Somewhat Disapprove
4. Strongly Disapprove

V31   Vote in 2008 General Election?
1. No
2. Yes

V32   Presidential Vote in 2008
1. Obama
2. McCain
3. Other

V33   Gun control should be made
1. More strict
2. Kept as is
3. Less Strict

V34   View about climate change
1. Global climate change has been established as a serious problem, and immediate action is necessary.

2. There is enough evidence that climate change is taking place, and some action should be taken.

3. We don't know enough about global climate change, and more research is necessary before we take any actions.

4. Concern about global climate change is exaggerated. No action is necessary.

5. Global climate change is not occurring; this is not a real issue.

V35   Grant legal status to illegal immigrants who have held jobs, paid taxes and no felony conviction
1. Yes
2. No

V36   Fine U.S. businesses that hire illegal immigrants
1. Yes
2. No

V37   Prohibit illegal immigrants from using emergency hospital care and public schools
1. Yes
2. No

V38   Deny automatic citizenship to American-born children of illegal immigrants
1. Yes
2. No

V39   View on abortion
1. By law, abortion should never be permitted
2. The law should permit abortion only in case of rape, incest, or when the woman's life is in danger
3. The law should permit abortion for reasons other than rape, incest, or danger to the woman's life, but only after the need for the abortion has been clearly established
4. By law, a woman should always be able to obtain an abortion as a matter of personal choice

V40   Which is closer to the way you feel, or haven't you thought much about this?
1. Much more important to protect environment even if lose jobs and lower standard of living
2. Environment somewhat more important

3. About the same
4. Economy somewhat more important
5. Much more important to protect jobs, even if environment worse

V41   Gay marriage
1. Favor
2. Oppose

V42   If Congress were to balance the budget, you would most prefer
1. Cut Defense Spending
2. Cut Domestic Spending
3. Raise Taxes

V43   Support Simpson-Bowles (15% across the board cuts, eliminate many tax breaks, reduce deficit by 21% by 2020)
1. Support
2. Oppose

V44   Extend Bush era tax cuts for incomes below $200,000—increase deficit by $205 billion?
1. Support
2. Oppose

V45   Extend Bush era tax cuts for everyone—increase deficit by $405 billion?
1. Support
2. Oppose

V46   Repeal Affordable Care Act?
1. Support
2. Oppose

V47   End "Don't Ask, Don't Tell"?
1. Support
2. Oppose

For each of the following, where would you place them on a 7-point ideology scale?
1. Very Liberal
2. Liberal
3. Somewhat Liberal

4. Middle of the Road
5. Somewhat Conservative
6. Conservative
7. Very Conservative

V48   Yourself

V49   Obama

V50   Romney

V51   Democratic Party

V52   Republican Party

V53   Tea Party Movement

POST-ELECTION

V54   Did you vote in 2012?
1. Yes
2. No

V55   Method of Voting
1. In person on election day
2. In person before election day (early)
3. Voted by mail (or absentee)
4. Don't know

V56   Presidential Vote 2012
1. Obama
2. Romney
3. Other

V57   U.S. Senate Vote 2012
1. Democratic candidate
2. Republican candidate
3. Other

V58   U.S. House Vote 2012
1. Democratic candidate
2. Republican candidate
3. Other

V59   Non-Voter Preference 2012
       1. Obama
       2. Romney
       3. Other

V60   If state had a budget deficit, what percent should come
       from tax increases and spending cuts (0–100)
       0. All tax increases
       . . .
       50. Equal
       . . .
       100. All cuts

V61   Did you put up a political sign in the last year?
       1. Yes
       2. No

V62   Make a political donation?
       1. Yes
       2. No

V63   Contributions made to all candidates and committees
       Actual value from $0 to $1 million

V64   Were you contacted by a candidate or political
       organization?
       1. Yes
       2. No

V65   The Irish, Italians, Jews, and many other minorities
       overcame prejudice and worked their way up. Blacks
       should do the same without any favors.
       1. Strongly agree
       2. Somewhat agree
       3. Neither agree nor disagree
       4. Somewhat disagree
       5. Strongly disagree

V66   View of Tea Party
       1. Very positive
       2. Somewhat positive
       3. Neutral
       4. Somewhat negative
       5. Very negative
       6. Don't know/No opinion

STATE NUMBERS

1. Alabama	21. Kentucky	38. North Dakota
2. Alaska	22. Louisiana	39. Ohio
4. Arizona	23. Maine	40. Oklahoma
5. Arkansas	24. Maryland	41. Oregon
6. California	25. Massachusetts	42. Pennsylvania
8. Colorado	26. Michigan	44. Rhode Island
9. Connecticut	27. Minnesota	45. South Carolina
10. Delaware	28. Mississippi	46. South Dakota
11. District of	29. Missouri	47. Tennessee
Columbia	30. Montana	48. Texas
12. Florida	31. Nebraska	49. Utah
13. Georgia	32. Nevada	50. Vermont
15. Hawaii	33. New	51. Virginia
16. Idaho	Hampshire	53. Washington
17. Illinois	34. New Jersey	54. West Virginia
18. Indiana	35. New Mexico	55. Wisconsin
19. Iowa	36. New York	56. Wyoming
20. Kansas	37. North Carolina	

▌A7: CROSSNAT CODEBOOK

From IDEA (latest year data exists 2010–2014) (http://www.idea.int/uid/).

IDEA_ESF   Electoral System Family
1. Proportional
2. Plurality/Majority
3. Mixed
4. Other

IDEA_ESNL_LH   Electoral System for National Legislature-Lower House
1. List Proportional
2. First Past the Post
3. Single Non-Transferable Vote
4. Single Transferable Vote
5. Alternative Vote
6. Block Vote
7. Party Block Vote
8. Mixed Member Proportional
9. Parallel Systems
10. Two Round System
11. Other

IDEA_ESNL_UH   Electoral System for National Legislature-Upper House
1. List Proportional
2. First Past the Post
3. Single Non-Transferable Vote
4. Single Transferable Vote
5. Alternative Vote
6. Block Vote
7. Party Block Vote
8. Mixed Member Proportional
9. Parallel Systems
10. Two Round System
11. Other
12. Appointed or Indirectly Elected

IDEA_ESP   Electoral System for President
2. First Past the Post
10. Two Round System
11. Other
12. Non-presidential system

IDEA_PT   Parliament Type
1. Bicameral
2. Unicameral

IDEA_SWLH   Percentage of Seats Held by Women in Lower House
IDEA_SWUH   Percentage of Seats Held by Women in Upper House
IDEA_DPFP   Provisions for Direct Public Funding to Political Parties
1. Yes
2. No

IDEA_FMP   Provisions for Free or Subsidized Access to Media for Political Parties
1. Yes
2. No

IDEA_FMC   Provisions for Free or Subsidized Access to Media for Candidates
1. Yes
2. No

IDEA_LPS   Limits on Party Spending
1. Yes
2. No

IDEA_LCS   Limits on Candidate Spending
1. Yes
2. No

CVOTE_L   Compulsory Voting-Legislature
1. Yes
2. No

CVOTE_P   Compulsory Voting-President
1. Yes
2. No

IDEA_VTR_PA	Percentage Voter Turnout Registered Voters-Parliament
IDEA_VTVAP_PA	Percentage Voter Turnout Voting Age Population-Parliament
IDEA_VTR_PR	Percentage Voter Turnout Registered Voters-President
IDEA_VTVAP_PR	Percentage Voter Turnout Voting Age Population-President

From the World Bank's WDI: 2012 data
http://data.worldbank.org/data-catalog/world-development-indicators/wdi-2012

WDI_DR	Death rate per 1,000 people
WDI_LEBM	Life expectancy at birth, female
WDI_LEBM	Life expectancy at birth, male
WDI_LEBM	Life expectancy at birth, total
WDI_65F	Survival to age 65, female (% of cohort)
WDI_65M	Survival to age 65, male (% of cohort)
WDI_IMF	Mortality rate, infant, female (per 1,000 live births)
WDI_IMM	Mortality rate, infant, male (per 1,000 live births)
WDI_IMT	Mortality rate, infant, total (per 1,000 live births)
WDI_LITF	Literacy rate, 15+, female
WDI_LITM	Literacy rate, 15+, male
WDI_LITT	Literacy rate, 15+, total
WDI_EF	Employment to population ratio, 15+, female
WDI_EM	Employment to population ratio, 15+, male
WDI_ET	Employment to population ratio, 15+, total
WDI_LFF	Labor force participation rate, total (% of total population ages 15+, female)
WDI_LFM	Labor force participation rate, total (% of total population ages 15+, male)
WDI_LFT	Labor force participation rate, total (% of total population ages 15+, total)
WDI_EX	Exports of goods and services (% of GDP)
WDI_IMP	Imports of goods and services (% of GDP)
WDI_GDP	GDP per capita (constant 2005 US$)
WDI_GNI	GNI per capita (constant 2005 US$)
WDI_GS	Gross savings (% of GDP)
WDI_UP	Urban population (% of total)
WDI_ME	Military expenditure (% of GDP)

| WDI_HE | Health expenditure per capita (current US$) |
| WDI_INT | Internet users (per 100 people) |

From Freedom House (total scales run from least to most free) 2012 data
http://www.freedomhouse.org/report/freedom-world-aggregate-and-subcategory-scores#.U-fj035EPwY
http://freedomhouse.org/report-types/freedom-press#.U-flIH5EPwY

FH_AF	Total Freedom Score (0–100) = FH_PR + FH_CL
FH_PR	Political Rights Total Score (0–40)
FH_CL	Civil Liberties Total Score (0–60)
FH_PF	Press Freedom Total Score (0–100)

From the Heritage Foundation (scales run 0 through 100, from least to most free)*
http://www.heritage.org/index/explore?view=by-region-country-year

HF_OV	Overall Score
HF_PR	Property Rights Freedom
HF_FC	Freedom from Corruption
HF_FF	Fiscal Freedom
HF_GS	Government Spending
HF_BF	Business Freedom
HF_LF	Labor Freedom
HF_MF	Monetary Freedom
HF_TF	Trade Freedom
HF_IF	Investment Freedom
HF_FIF	Financial Freedom
HF_CTR	Corporate Tax Rate
HF_TB	Tax Burden as %GDP
HF_GE	Government Expenditure as %GDP
HF_GDP5	5 Year Growth in GDP
HF_GDPPC	GDP per Capita
HF_UNEMP	Unemployment %
HF_INFLATE	Inflation %

*Data mainly covering period from 2012 to 2013. For full explanation of data and scales see
http://www.freedomhouse.org/reports#.U-FPRxFEPwY
http://www.heritage.org/index/about

NOTE

1   Means and medians for all feeling thermometer entries calculated after WEIGHT=PW applied.

Appendix B

An Example of a Term-Wide Set of Computer Exercises—ANES2012A

Instructor's note: Although these exercises are broken into three alternative possibilities for your students to choose, you can actually break these down into nine possible combinations of independent and dependent variables. This may be most helpful for those of you with large classes with multiple discussion sections.

EXERCISE 1: TRIAL RUN—OPENING A DATA SET

COMMANDS NEEDED:

- **WEIGHT**
- **FREQUENCIES**

Task 1: Open your **ANES2012A.SAV** data set as specified in Chapter 1.
Task 2: Either by way of syntax or **GUI** commands:

- Weight the data by **PW2012**
- Run a simple frequency distribution for **V1** (gender)

Data check:

You should have produced a table with 48% classified as males, 52% as females (N = 2,056).

EXERCISE 2: VISUALIZING DATA

COMMANDS NEEDED:

- **WEIGHT**
- **COMPUTE**
- **FREQUENCIES**

Reasoning: Before we can even start to examine tests for our hypotheses, we need to understand how and if we are correctly measuring our properties. "Massaging" data in a theoretically responsible way is a key tool for analysis (and one that is marketable). Visualizing data is also a helpful tool for presenting our findings to others.

Task 1: Open up the **ANES2012A SPSS** data file (as you did in the TRIAL RUN). As before, use **PW2012** as your weight.

Task 2: Run a simple frequency distribution for one of the following dichotomous variables. They will be used in Exercise 3:

V*46* Favor/oppose death penalty
V*47* Make buying a gun more difficult or not
V*22* Does one have health insurance?

Task 3: Display and describe your findings. "Display" by showing the frequency distribution that will automatically be produced with a bar chart and a pie chart (see example 4.6, page 55). In order to produce both, *do not* include (as in the manual) **/FORMAT= NOTABLE** as that would eliminate the frequency distribution listing.

Task 4: **COMPUTE** (section 3.2) three new variables comparing feeling thermometers towards the Democratic Party and its candidates with those thermometers for Republicans.

PRESDIFF (V*16*-V*17*)
PARTYDIFF (V*18*-V*19*)
VPDIFF (V*71*-V*72*)

1. For each, what does a positive number mean?
2. For each, what does a negative number mean?
3. For each, what does "0" mean?

Task 5: Display, with three separate bar charts, these three feeling thermometer differences. Use the **FREQUENCIES** procedure, but suppress your actual distribution table (**FORMAT=NOTABLE**). From the chart produced, what is your general impression or assessment of the differences produced for *each* of those distributions?

Task 6: Quickly make a general claim about the similarities/differences among those three difference measures. Which one seems to be most skewed towards the Democratic Party or candidate?

A note on "feeling thermometers": a rating of "0" indicates that one has the most negative feeling possible towards a candidate, a 100 the most positive, and 50 is completely neutral.

EXERCISE 3: MEANS

COMMANDS NEEDED:

WEIGHT
COMPUTE
MEANS

In the second exercise, you were asked to use several **SPSS** commands to transform, create, and visualize certain variables in your **ANES2012A** data set. In this exercise, you will continue the analysis with a more formal statistical summary of the data.

Task 1: Open up the **ANES2012A SPSS** data file (as you did in the TRIAL RUN). As before, use **PW2012** as your weight.

Task 2: Create the variables **PRESDIFF**, **PARTYDIFF**, and **VPDIFF** as you did before.

Task 3: Use the variable you chose in Exercise 1 as your independent (explanatory) variable:

V46 Favor/oppose death penalty
V47 Make buying a gun more difficult or not
V22 Does one have health insurance?

Using the **MEANS** procedure (Chapter 4.2), generate the mean, median, standard deviation, range, and raw count (N) for your computed variables **PRESDIFF**, **PARTYDIFF** and **VPDIFF** for each (2) of your independent variable categories. Use the example 7.1 as your guide, *BUT CHANGE* the dependent variables (*not* V72) and independent variable (*not* V1). I'll leave this part up to you.

Task 4: Compare and fully interpret the differences between your two independent variable categories in terms of their means, medians, standard deviations, and ranges of your three dependent variables.

Task 5: Using information about the means and medians, does your analysis confirm/disconfirm the following hypothesis (choose the one that goes along with your independent variable)?

Individuals who favor the death penalty are more likely to lean Republican than those who are opposed.

Individuals who believe it should be more difficult to buy a gun are more likely to lean Democratic than those who believe the rules should stay the same or be made easier.

Individuals with health insurance are more likely to lean Democratic than those without.

Task 6: Compare the results you obtained with **PRESDIFF, PARTY-DIFF,** and **VPDIFF.** Which one does your independent variable **(V46 or V47 or V22)** seem to have a greater effect on? Verbally interpret that difference and what you think may be going on with the 2012 electorate.

EXERCISE 4: T-TESTS

COMMANDS NEEDED:

- **WEIGHT**
- **COMPUTE**
- **T-TEST**

In the third exercise, you were asked to compare the differences between the means of your two independent variable categories *descriptively.* This time, however, you will use the set of **T-TEST commands** to conduct inferential hypothesis tests of differences on those variables. Use the examples in Chapter 4.3 for examples of syntax, **GUIs,** and interpretation.

Task 1: Open up the **ANES2012A SPSS** data file (as you did in the TRIAL RUN). As before, use **PW2012** as your weight.

Task 2: Create the variables **PRESDIFF, PARTYDIFF,** and **VPDIFF** as you did before.

Task 3: Using the **T-TEST TESTVAL** procedure, determine whether you can *confidently reject* the possibility that, in the population from which the **NES** sample was drawn, there is no difference in mean feelings toward the presidential candidates (**PRESDIFF**), the parties (**PARTYDIFF**), and the Vice Presidential candidates (**VPDIFF**). Set **TESTVAL** to 0.

Explain why or why not.

Translation: Is there truly a difference in the population between your two independent variable categories on each of those difference scales or may the difference you computed be attributed to the random luck of the draw? Is the sample mean thermometer differences calculated significantly different enough from "0" degrees (no mean difference between the two presidential candidates and/or parties and/or vice presidential candidates) to confidently reject "0" degrees as a possibility?

Relevant findings: Refer to the following from your output to answer that question: t-value, significance of the t-test value, and the 95% confidence interval values.

Data check: Make sure that the sample mean calculated with the **T-TEST** procedures are as follows:

PRESDIFF=8.8294 (N=2021)
PARTYDIFF=8.1373 (N=2013)
VPDIFF==2.4803 (N=1701)

Task 4: Use the variable you chose in Exercise 1 as your independent (explanatory) variable:

V*46* Favor/oppose death penalty
V*47* Make buying a gun more difficult or not
V*22* Does one have health insurance?

Using the **T-TEST GROUPS** procedure, compare and interpret the **PRESDIFF** means of your two independent variable groups: Groups (categories 1 and 2). Are those mean differences significantly different from each other in the sample to confidently reject the possibility that the mean difference in the population between your two groups equals 0 degrees? Why or why not?

Translation: Is there truly a difference in the population between your two groups or may the difference we computed be attributed to the random luck of the draw? Is the sample mean difference calculated between your two sample groups on **PRESDIFF** significantly different enough from "0" degrees (no mean difference between the groups) to confidently reject "0" degrees as a possibility in the population from which the sample was drawn?

Data check: Make sure that the sample means calculated with this **T-TEST** procedure are as follows.

	Group 1	Group 2
V46	–1.1900	30.0833
V47	30.8872	–8.3796
V22	6.1178	24.4452

Relevant findings: Refer to the following from your output to answer that question: t-value, significance of the t-test value, and the 95% confidence interval values. Use the more conservative "Equal variances not assumed" figures.

Task 5: Using the **T-TEST PAIRS** procedure, determine whether you can *confidently reject* the possibility that, in the population from which this **ANES** sample was drawn, there is no difference in the mean values of **PRESDIFF** and **PARTYDIFF**. Explain why or why not.

Translation: Is there truly a difference in the population between these two variables means or may the difference we computed be attributed to the random luck of the draw? Is the sample mean difference calculated between **PRESDIFF** and **PARTYDIFF** significantly different enough from "0" degrees (no mean difference between the variables) to confidently reject "0" degrees as a possibility in the population?

Data check: Make sure that the sample means calculated with this **T-TEST** procedure for **PRESDIFF=9.2304*** and for **PARTYDIFF=8.0082.**

*The means are different from what you should have found in task 2.

Reason: In task 2 all 2,021 respondents for whom there was a difference in evaluation between the presidential candidates were included, as were all 2,013 who responded to **PARTYDIFF**. In this step, only those for whom a difference could be included for *both* **PRESDIFF** and **PARTYDIFF** are included (N = 1,992).

Relevant findings: Refer to the following from your output to answer that question: t-value, significance of the t-test value, and the 95% confidence interval values.

Extra Task 6: Perform a similar analysis for the differences between **PRESDIFF** and **VPDIFF** and between **PARTYDIFF** and **VPDIFF**.

EXERCISE 5: CROSSTABS

COMMANDS NEEDED:

- **WEIGHT**
- **COMPUTE**
- **RECODE**
- **FREQUENCIES**
- **CROSSTABS**

In the third and fourth exercises, you were asked to compare the differences between the means of your two independent variable categories *descriptively* and then *inferentially*. This time, you will use

CROSSTABS to conduct a similar test of differences on those variables, but you will first collapse your interval level thermometer difference scales into three ordinal categories. Use the CROSSTABS examples in Chapter 4.5 for examples of syntax, GUIs, and interpretation.

Task 1: Open up the ANES2012A SPSS data file (as you did in the TRIAL RUN). As before, use PW2012 as your weight.

Task 2: Create the variables PRESDIFF, PARTYDIFF, and VPDIFF as you did before.

Task 3: Recode each of those three variables (separately) into three new variables:

PRES3, PARTY3, VP3

Collapse your three original variables into just three categories:

- leans towards the Republicans (–1): -100 thru –1
- same feeling thermometer rating for both parties (0): 0
- leans towards the Democrats (+1): +1 thru 100.

Data check: Before you go any further, make sure that your frequency distributions for PRES3, PARTY3, and VP3 are as follows:

PRES3

		Frequency	Percent	Valid Percent	Cumulative Percent
Valid	-1.00	778	37.9	38.5	38.5
	.00	159	7.7	7.9	46.4
	1.00	1084	52.7	53.6	100.0
	Total	2021	98.3	100.0	
Missing	System	35	1.7		
Total		2056	100.0		

PARTY3

		Frequency	Percent	Valid Percent	Cumulative Percent
Valid	-1.00	716	34.8	35.6	35.6
	.00	366	17.8	18.2	53.7
	1.00	931	45.3	46.3	100.0
	Total	2013	97.9	100.0	
Missing	System	43	2.1		
Total		2056	100.0		

VP3

		Frequency	Percent	Valid Percent	Cumulative Percent
Valid	-1.00	665	32.4	39.1	39.1
	.00	269	13.1	15.8	54.9
	1.00	767	37.3	45.1	100.0
	Total	1701	82.8	100.0	
Missing	System	355	17.2		
Total		2056	100.0		

Task 4: Using the **CROSSTABS** procedure , create a 3 × 2 table with *your* previously chosen independent variable (**V46, V47,** or **V22**) as your independent variable (columns), **PRES3, PARTY3,** and **VP3,** individually, as your dependent variable (rows). Ask for column percentages, chi-square, lambda, and Cramer's V.

Task 5: Answer the following questions

  ▨ Which of your two independent variable groups is more likely to lean towards Democratic candidate Obama? By what percentage point difference?

  ▨ Which of your two independent variable groups is more likely to lean towards the Democratic Party? By what percentage point difference?

  ▨ Which of your two independent variable groups is more likely to lean towards the Democrat VP candidate Biden? By what percentage point difference?

Task 6: Using lambda, how well does *your* independent variable descriptively predict one's candidate and party leanings?

Task 7: Using Cramer's V, how strong is the correlation between your independent variable and your dependent variables?

Task 8: Using chi-square (Pearson), given the differences in this sample, can you confidently claim that some leaning difference between your two independent variable groups on each of your dependent variables (difference > 0%) also exists in the population from which this sample was (randomly) drawn? Why or why not?

Task 9: Compare your results from Exercise 4 and Exercise 5. Does the type of analysis and the reclassification of categories make any difference in how you respond to the hypotheses listed in Exercise 3?

Individuals who favor the death penalty are more likely to lean Republican than those who are opposed.

Individuals who believe it should be more difficult to buy a gun are more likely to lean Democratic than those who believe the rules should stay the same or be made easier.

Individuals with health insurance are more likely to lean Democratic than those without.

EXERCISE 6: USING REGRESSIONS

COMMANDS NEEDED:

- **WEIGHT**
- **COMPUTE**
- **REGRESSION**

You will finish this set of exercises by employing a linear regression model to test for the relationships between a new variable and your three dependent variables.

Task 1: Open up the **ANES2012A SPSS** data file. As before, use **PW2012** as your weight.

Task 2: Create the variables **PRESDIFF, PARTYDIFF,** and **VPDIFF** as you did before.

Task 3: Using the **REGRESSON** command, test the linear relationship between the **PARTYDIFF** (this will serve as your independent variable) and, separately, each of your other two dependent variables (**PRESDIFF** and **VPDIFF**). For which dependent variable is **PARTYDIFF** a better explanatory fit?

Task 4: Interpret both the intercepts and slopes of your two regression equations.

Task 5: Use *your* chosen independent variable (**V46, V47,** or **V22**) as a dummy variable and add it to the equation. Reinterpret your intercepts and slopes.

Task 6: Is your dummy variable more or less important in explaining the variance of **PRESDIFF** and **VPDIFF** than **PARTYDIFF**? Does it add anything to your explanation?

Task 7: Using the **/SELECT** subcommand for **REGRESSION**, produce two regression equations (one for each of *your* independent variable choices). Answer the following:

- For which of your two categories is **PARTYDIFF** a better explanatory fit for **PRESDIFF**?
- Interpret the intercept and slope for each of your regressions.

EXERCISE 7:

Using the results and interpretations produced in Exercises 2–6, summarize your findings.